METAFRAME ®
TROPICAL
AQUARIUM FISHES
FRESHWATER & MARINE

METAFRAME ®
TROPICAL
AQUARIUM FISHES
FRESHWATER & MARINE

unicom
New York,

CONTENTS

Published for The Metaframe Aquarium Book Club
by Unicom Publishing Corp.,
40 West 57th Street, New York, N.Y. 10019
Copyright © 1972 The Hamlyn Publishing Group Ltd.
Printed in the U.S.A.

FRESHWATER FISHES

GEORGE CUST

MANAGEMENT OF THE FRESHWATER AQUARIUM

The common freshwater tropical fish is a hardy creature and on the whole adapts very well to the environmental changes to which it is subjected in the aquarium. This type of fish is kept by thousands of aquarists who have never measured the hardness or pH of the water in their fish tanks, but to keep the more delicate species or to breed the more difficult egg-layers the aquarist may have to modify the environmental conditions. A basic understanding of water chemistry will help him to carry out these modifications successfully.

WATER

Paradoxically the source of fresh water is the sea. The sun causes evaporation from its surface which, as water vapour, rises into the atmosphere and forms clouds. When clouds cool, their water vapour may be precipitated as rain which picks up various impurities as it falls through the atmosphere. These are very few if the rain is falling on rural areas but over towns it picks up carbon dioxide, sulphur dioxide, hydrocarbons, tars and dust particles.

Once on the ground the water may dissolve chemicals from the soil and the rocks through which it passes. In limestone areas the water will dissolve calcium salts and become hard (temporary hardness) or may dissolve magnesium salts and become hard (permanent hardness). The main quality that most people notice about hard water is that it will not lather soap properly and that it furs up kettles, but from the fish-keeping point of few, some fishes prefer soft water, for example killifishes and characins, whereas others, such as the Australian Rainbow (*Melanotaenia nigrans*) and the Lake Nyasa cichlids, prefer hard water.

Public water supplies which come from deep wells are usually hard; water which comes from surface reservoirs on moors and mountains is usually soft. In the process of purifying water for human consumption the public water companies subject the water to a number of chemical and mechanical processes. Minute amounts of some of these chemicals remain in the water but the only one of importance to the freshwater fish keeper is chlorine, added to most public water supplies as a disinfectant. Chlorine in the free state disperses if left standing in the aquarium for twenty-four hours and fishes, therefore, should not be put into newly filled aquaria. Most freshwater tropical fish keepers use tap water and this is satisfactory for keeping most fishes. For some species, however, and this is mentioned in the catalogue section under the appropriate entry, the water must be soft—or in rarer cases hard—to keep the fishes in the best condition and to breed them successfully.

Hardness can be measured in three different units: Clark's degrees (grains of calcium carbonate—$CaCO_3$—per UK gallon); German degrees DH (parts of CaO per 100,000); or in parts per 1,000,000 of $CaCO_3$ present in the water (ppm). The latter scale will be used throughout this book. For comparative purposes 14 ppm is approximately one Clark's degree or 0·8 DH.

Classification of water by ppm scale

Description of water	ppm
Soft	0–50
Medium soft	50–150
Hard	150–300
Very hard	Over 300

Local water companies will supply information on the hardness of the water in their area.

Gravel containing limestone or limestone rockwork will increase the hardness of water in the aquarium. The aquarist can measure the hardness of his tank water by the E.D.T.A. (Schwarzenbach) Method. This test can be carried out by any aquarist who has studied simple chemistry at school. Chemicals for this test are available from most suppliers of laboratory chemicals.

If the local water supply is hard, soft water may be obtained by collecting rainwater in plastic containers from glass or plastic roofs via plastic pipes, providing the aquarist lives in an area with relatively unpolluted air. Metal roofs or pipes may cause contamination. Hard water can be softened by ion-exchange resins giving demineralized water, or very expensive distilled water may be purchased. Temporary hardness may be removed by boiling the water and filtering off the precipitated calcium carbonate. These soft waters are better aerated for a few hours before placing fishes in them.

The acidity or alkalinity of the water he uses is another

chemical factor very important to the aquarist. This depends upon the concentration of hydrogen ions present in the water, of which the pH value is the measure. Neutral water has a pH of 7, strong alkalis a pH of 14, and strong acids a pH of 1. Water for fish keeping is within the limits of pH 4 to pH 9.

Most fishes which prefer soft water also prefer it to be acid and water may be acidified by adding peat. It is not recommended to add the peat directly to the tank as, although it sinks to the bottom after a few days, it is easily swished about by the fishes; it is better to add the peat to the aquarium filter. Use a good sphagnum peat moss and boil it in soft water for five minutes. Squeeze out and discard the surplus water (this contains excess humic acid

from the peat) and put the peat in the filter between two layers of filter wool. Running the filter gradually acidifies the aquarium water.

There are a number of fishes which live at the mouths of rivers, in coastal waters and estuaries, where the water is brackish. Some authorities recommend the addition of one teaspoonful of salt (NaCl) per gallon of water when keeping these species in the aquarium. Examples of such fishes are the Scat or Argus (*Scatophagus argus*), the Green Puffer Fish (*Tetraodon fluviatilis*) and the bumble bee fishes (*Brachygobius* species).

EQUIPMENT
Tanks The best shape for fish tanks is rectangular with the length two, three or four times greater than the depth. This gives the most common size of fish tank as

Glass Catfish (*Kryptopterus bicirrhus*)

$24 \times 12 \times 12$ in $(60 \times 30 \times 30$ cm), although larger sizes— $36 \times 12 \times 12$ in $(90 \times 30 \times 30$ cm) and $48 \times 12 \times 12$ in $(120 \times 30 \times 30$ cm)—are also common. The smallest size for a community of small fishes is $18 \times 10 \times 10$ in $(45 \times 25 \times 25$ cm). Tanks of this shape offer a large surface area in relation to depth and allow carbon dioxide expired by the fishes to be given off to the atmosphere easily.

Smaller tanks can be moulded completely in glass or plastic but the large tanks have angle iron or stainless steel frames into which the glass is fixed. The angle iron must be painted to stop it rusting. The upper surface of the angle iron on which the tank cover rests is most susceptible to rust and a good technique to prevent this is to rub down the paint on the top surface as soon as a new tank is bought and to paint the bare metal with two coats of a cold galvanizing paint, finishing off with two coats of good enamel paint in the same colour as the rest of the tank. The stainless steel and nylon-coated angle iron tanks are both trouble-free in this respect. Home-made, all-glass aquaria, in which synthetic bonding agents are used to fix the glass together, are another recent innovation.

Always put a glass cover on top of the tank; as well as preventing fishes leaping out and evaporation, it stops dust from gaining access. There are various tank covers which can be placed on top of the cover glass to house the lighting arrangements.

Heating The majority of tropical fishes are happy at a temperature of 72–78°F (22–26°C). Most aquarists use the conventional immersed heater and separate immersed thermostat to provide this controlled temperature. The immersed thermostats are of two main types; one is completely submersible and can be used in very shallow tanks but has to be taken out of the water to alter its setting, and the other has a control at the top which projects over the top of the tank. This type, therefore, cannot be completely submerged but alterations to its setting are easily made. External thermostats are also popular—these are either stuck or fixed by a stainless steel clip to the side glass of the aquarium. They have the advantage that their setting can be easily altered.

In recent years a few aquarists have used a base heating system employing the metal-encased electric heater used for greenhouse heating. This heater is placed about 2 in (5 cm) under the tank and is connected to an external thermostat, thus avoiding wires or heaters inside the tank. Combined submersible heater-thermostats are gaining in popularity.

Thermometers These are basically of two sorts; those using the bimetal strip mechanism or those using alcohol or mercury. The best type for the aquarium is a mercury thermometer with the scale marked directly on the glass. Nevertheless, the experienced aquarist develops the habit of touching the front of the tank with the back of his hand, for with practice he can tell if the temperature is 'right'—thermometers have been known to go wrong.

Lighting Ordinary light bulbs, allowing 25 watts per square foot of water surface area, for eight to twelve hours per day will give adequate lighting. The length of time depends upon the amount of daylight falling on the tank and the plants the aquarist wants to grow.

Fluorescent lighting is becoming popular and in recent years tubes emitting light of special wavelengths have been specially developed for aquarium use. There have been criticisms of these tubes and the latest idea is to use both a fluorescent tube and incandescent bulbs at the same time. Although fluorescent tubes are more expensive initially than ordinary bulbs, in the long term they are more economical because of their greater efficiency and longer life.

Aeration and filtration Aeration by passing a stream of air bubbles through the water helps to oxygenate it, mainly by agitating the surface and allowing a better exchange of oxygen and carbon dioxide. It also helps to cause circulation of water within the tank. A good stream of bubbles is easily produced by using an electrically driven pump and an air stone. The only real advantage of aeration is in tanks which are overcrowded and the normal aquarium should not need this aid.

Filtration filters from the water of the aquarium any particulate matter suspended in it and thus helps to keep the water crystal clear. However, not all fishes like a crystal clear tank; many of the catfishes, for example, like a layer of sediment on the bottom. If the filter material contains active charcoal some of the other chemicals, including waste products produced by the fishes, are also removed. Modern filters help provide a brisk circulation of water in the tank which fishes from running water enjoy but those from still water dislike.

Filters are of two main types, the box filter in which dirt is removed from the aquarium and the undergravel filter in which the sediment is sucked down into the gravel and subsequently broken up by bacterial action. Some aquarists believe undergravel filters interfere with the growth of aquarium plants.

PLANTS
One of the advantages of tropical freshwater tanks is that the aquarist can grow plants in them. The function of plants in the aquarium is to provide decoration and hiding places, and to give shade in some areas of the tank.

Tropical freshwater plants – 1 Floating Fern; 2 Cryptocoryne; 3 Amazon Sword; 4 Cabomba; 5 Valisneria

Although plants give off oxygen during the daylight hours, this oxygen is small in proportion to the amount that is transmitted through the surface layer of a properly shaped aquarium.

The genus *Cryptocoryne* consists of a number of favourite aquarium plants. They are bog plants in their natural condition in South-east Asia but they also grow very well when submerged. One of the most popular is *C. affinis*, which can grow up to 12 in (30 cm) tall. *C. beckettii* is another similar plant but not as fast growing. *C. blassii*, which is a very intense dark red under the leaf, is a more recently discovered *Cryptocoryne*, growing in popularity. Most of the members of this genus do not insist on bright light but do better in soft acid water. There are a number of small-sized species such as *C. nevillii*, which only grows to 2 in (5 cm).

The genus *Echinodorus* comes from America and also contains broad-leafed plants. *E. paniculatus*, the Amazon Sword Plant, is a popular species, but needs more light than the Cryptocorynes to grow well.

There are a number of fine-leafed plants such as *Cabomba caroliniana* and *Myriophyllum brasiliense* which are very attractive but in my experience either grow so well that they continually need thinning or never grow at all.

The species with grass-like leaves, *Vallisneria spiralis* and *Sagittaria* species, for example, are also attractive and popular plants. Both genera grow well in well-lighted aquaria with ordinary aquarium gravel as compost.

The floating or top plants such as *Lemna* species (Duckweed) or *Salvinia* species do not grow well under artificial light. The two species of the genus *Ceratopteris* (Floating Fern), however, do very well under artificial light and their roots and leaves are very useful as a place for the Anabantidae to anchor their bubble nests.

DECOR

Every tropical fish hobbyist should have one tank which he sets up with the intention of creating a beautiful and attractive piece of furniture in his home. This tank should be at least $24 \times 12 \times 12$ in ($60 \times 30 \times 30$ cm) and preferably larger so that he has scope for aquascaping.

For this furnished aquarium it is a good idea to paint the ends and back of the tank black on the outside to provide a background which sets off the colours of the plants and fishes. Choose an attractively coloured gravel of a particle size of about $\frac{1}{8}$—$\frac{3}{16}$ in (3–5 mm), and even though the gravel is sold as well washed, always wash it

again. Choose your rockwork carefully; it is possible to buy rockwork but it is far better to find your own on the mountains, on rocky shorelines or in mountain streams. My furnished aquarium has some beautiful red sandstone rocks found on the shore of the Isle of Skye. Do not use limestone rockwork in your tank.

Plants are now needed to set the scene for the fishes. Aquascaping is a very personal choice and I prefer to use only Cryptocorynes—they do not require excessive light, they grow reasonably slowly so that the 'picture' in the tank remains unchanging, and there is not the constant necessity of having to thin out plants as with faster-growing species. It is a good idea before setting up a furnished aquarium to have a look at other aquarists' tanks and at show tanks at major fish shows to find out what appeals to you.

Finally the fishes are added, preferably all more or less of the same size and chosen so that they will all live together peaceably. It is a good idea never to have just one fish of a species; if you have a few they always stimulate each other to better colour and more interesting behaviour. It is also advisable to have one species more numerous than the rest, one of the small tetras, for example, such as the Cardinal Tetra (*Cheirodon axelrodi*) or Glowlight Tetra (*Hemigrammus gracilis*), as these species shoal together so well. Include some live-bearers —Red Platies (*Xiphophorus maculatus*) or Swordtails (*X. helleri*) look well against the black background—and also a couple of Sucking Loaches (*Gyrinocheilus aymonieri*). These are not chosen for their looks but because they will act as vacuum cleaners and keep algae from growing on the glass and plants.

Fishes are best fed daily, and at the same time the hobbyist can check that they all look well and healthy and also on the temperature of the water and that it looks clear. About every three to four weeks the front glass may need to be scraped with a razor blade scraper if algae are found growing there. From time to time it may be necessary to siphon off any collection of mulm on the bottom and to top up the water to replace evaporation losses. This is a lot less care and attention than most other pets require and fishes do not suffer damage if left unattended for two to three weeks when the aquarist is away on holiday—fishes in good condition come to no harm if left without food for this period of time.

FOODS AND NUTRITION

Fishes need proteins, fats, carbohydrates, vitamins and minerals in their diet to keep them in good health and colour and to keep them growing. Some fishes in the wild are predominantly herbivores, as the silver dollars (*Myloplus* species), which need lettuce or spinach added to their diet in the aquarium, while others are predominantly carnivores, for example the Pike Top Minnow (*Belonesox belizanus*), which eat other fishes, dragonfly larvae, tadpoles and worms. There are other fishes, however, which are less demanding and will eat all live foods and a wide variety of dried foods and chopped liver. To ensure that the fish gets the essential amino acids (the basic structure of proteins) it needs and sufficient vitamins and minerals, as wide a range of foodstuffs as possible should be offered. This also helps to reduce the monotony of a one-food diet since fishes, like humans, do seem to become bored with the same food every day. Occasionally fishes which have been fed predominantly on one type of food almost seem to get addicted to this one type and will eat no other. This should be prevented by offering a wide range of foodstuffs, since the food for which the fishes have an addiction may at some time or other be difficult to obtain.

LIVE FOODS
Pond life The first group are natural foods found in freshwater ponds: the Freshwater Shrimp (*Gammarus pulex*) and the water louse (*Asellus*), which can only be taken by the larger fishes; the water fleas, the most common of which are *Daphnia* and *Cyclops*; and the larvae of various insects. Mosquito and midge larvae particularly are excellent foods. These live foods contain proteins, fats, oils, minerals and vitamins and are foods which many fishes eat in their natural habitat. It is also food which has to be chased and caught by the fish and is, therefore, probably enjoyed all the more.

These foods have also to be caught by the aquarist. Equipped with a large fine-mesh net with a long handle, he must go and find out what his local ponds yield. Usually such foods as *Cyclops* can only be caught in large numbers in the spring and summer months, but these foods are very good for fishes. The first good feed of *Daphnia* in spring seems to be their signal that winter has ended and the breeding season has come round again.

There is, however, one drawback to these foods: *Hydra*, leeches, or the larvae of carnivorous insects can be introduced into the fish tank with the *Daphnia* if one is not careful. Dragon fly larvae, for example, will eat fishes bigger than themselves, but *Hydra* are only dangerous to newly hatched fry and soon die out in a tank if *Daphnia* are not fed; hungry fishes will also eat *Hydra*. Careful examination will prevent dragonfly larvae and leeches from being put into the tank with *Daphnia*. It is

Female *Daphnia* with young in pouch

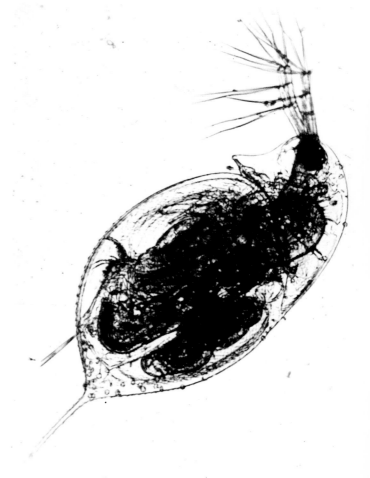

also possible that some freshwater crustacea are capable of being infected by fungi such as *Ichthyosporidium* and infection can be transmitted to fishes when the crustacea are eaten.

Tubifex worms (Family Tubificidae) These are red worms which live in mud at the edges of rivers and ponds, the tail of the worm only sticking out of the mud. They are a good food but as many of them come from sewage-contaminated water there is a danger of their introducing bacteria, fungal and virus infection into the tank, so it is better to buy them already cleaned from pet stores. Even so they are best put in a large bowl or bucket and kept under a slow-running tap for twenty-four hours before being fed to fishes.

Earthworms (*Lumbricus*) These are a very good food and the smaller red worms are best. These can be fed whole to large fishes or chopped or shredded into pieces of appropriate size for smaller ones. The only disadvantages for the aquarist are that he has to dig up his own earthworms and chopping them up can be a very messy business.

Whiteworms (*Enchytraeus albidus*) These are much smaller relatives of the earthworm and can be cultivated by the aquarist so that he has a year-round supply. They are good sources of protein and fat but are, perhaps, short in some vitamins as there have been reports of fishes which have been fed exclusively on Whiteworms for many months ceasing to grow and being in poor condition.

A wooden box about 12 × 6 × 3 in (30 × 15 × 7.5 cm) is required; it should not be too well made, so that excess water can drain out through the joints if necessary. This should be filled with a compost formed by a mixture of fifty per cent peat and fifty per cent leafmould (obtainable from garden shops) and watered until it looks and feels moist. The Whiteworm culture (from other aquarists or pet shops) can then be added and finally a shallow depression about 2 in (5 cm) in diameter is made on the surface of the compost in which to put the food for the worms. Any cereal food made for babies mixed into a sloppy mixture with water is good for feeding Whiteworms. The box should be covered with a glass and kept in a dark place, at about 55°F (13°C), which is the ideal temperature.

The worms come to the surface to feed and may be collected with tweezers. Once a month empty out the whole box on to a sheet of paper and break up and mix all the compost together before it is put back into the box. This aerates the compost and greatly aids the multiplication of the worms.

DRIED FOODS

These are available from all pet shops and many of them are specially formulated and contain vitamin supplements. It is best to try out a few different sorts until finding the one which suits your own fishes best. Only feed as much dried food at a time as the fishes eat within five minutes, for uneaten food will decompose and pollute the tank. Freeze-dried *Tubifex* is also available.

LIVER

This is a very good, cheap, basic food. Boil ox liver for five minutes and then put it in the freezer compartment of the refrigerator for twenty-four hours. It can then be minced or shredded into smaller pieces with a small kitchen mincer or blender and kept in jars in the freezer for future use. It will keep for up to three months.

VEGETABLE FOODS

Some fishes must have plant food in their diet and many like this occasionally. Large fishes like *Metynnis* species will eat shredded lettuce, others like the mollies (*Mollienesia* species) will eat spinach (use frozen shredded spinach). Even characins seem to enjoy a cooked pea squashed into their tank water.

FOODS FOR FRY

An emulsion of egg yolk is very good as the first food for the small fry of egg-layers. Hard boil an egg and put a piece about $\frac{1}{4}$ in (6 mm) in diameter into a jam jar full of water, rubbing the yolk between finger and thumb to get it into the water as a fine suspension. Add this to the water in small amounts about three times a day. The fry eat the egg yolk particles and the egg encourages the growth of infusoria (protozoa) in the water on which the fish will also feed. These protozoa, the most common of which is *Paramecium*, are present in small numbers in all tanks and multiply rapidly when fed in this way. Commercial first foods for fry are also very successful. These consist of emulsions of various proteins with added preservative and produce a cloud of fine particles when added to water.

When the fry get larger they can be fed newly hatched Brine Shrimp (*Artemia salina*). Brine Shrimp eggs are sold by all pet shops and can be hatched out within forty-eight hours by incubating at 80°F (27°C) in a salt solution (two level teaspoons per pint of water—or use sea water if you can get it). One system which works very well is to have two shallow trays 12 × 6 × 3 in (30 × 15 × 7.5 cm). Filter off the shrimps through a fine cloth and rinse them into the tank.

Micro-worms (*Anguilluda silusia*) are another good and useful food. Obtain an initial culture from the pet shop or a fellow aquarist. Make a culture medium by mixing up baby cereal food with water to form a stiff mixture and put this into a plastic box about 3 × 3 in (7.5 × 7.5 cm) to a depth of $\frac{1}{2}$ in (1 cm) and add the culture. It is a good idea to place a small piece of polystyrene about 1 in (2.5 cm) square by $\frac{1}{4}$ in (6 mm) deep on the surface of the culture medium before covering with a lid. After about four days of growth at a temperature of 70–80°F (21–27°C) the worms, which are only $\frac{1}{8}$ in (3 mm) long, swarm up the sides of the box and on to the polystyrene and can be taken off with a small moist brush. The culture goes sour after about seven days and should be replaced by innoculating some new medium from the old culture.

As the fry grow larger they can be given sifted *Daphnia* and *Cyclops*, and chopped Whiteworm and *Tubifex*.

ANATOMY AND PHYSIOLOGY OF FISHES

FINS

There are two main groups of fins, the unpaired kind—the dorsal, the anal and the caudal fins—and the paired kind—the pectoral (the equivalent of arms in animals) and the pelvic fins (in the position of legs in other animals). The fins are made up of rays, the first ones in some species being hard and the remainder soft. The number of soft and hard rays is used in species identification.

The unpaired fins serve as stabilizers and help to direct the fish the way it wants to go. The caudal fin is an important source of propulsion, while the pectoral fins are used for slow movement, particularly for hanging motionless in the water. In some fishes, which are good

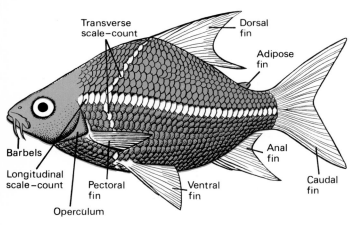

External features of a fish

leapers, these fins are particularly large. The pelvic fins are used as stabilizers.

SKIN

The skin of the fish consists of two main layers, the epidermis and the deeper dermis. Scales, which are a form of external skeleton, are developed from the dermis. Most of the living species of Osteichthys (bony fishes—the class to which most aquarium species belong) have a bony ridge type of scale which is thin and translucent, the outer surface showing alternate bony ridges and depressions. Scale characteristics are also important in the classification of different genera and species of fishes.

The number of scales on the length of the body from gill cover (operculum) to caudal fin along the lateral line (longitudinal scale count) and at the greatest point of body depth (transverse scale count) are constant in each species of fish and are helpful in identification.

Situated also in the dermis are mucous glands, the secretions of which give the characteristic slimy touch and odour to a fish. The mucus probably lessens the drag on a fish as it swims through the water and helps to protect it against infections.

The colour of fishes is largely due to pigments in the skin, although there is some background colour from the colour of the underlying tissues and blood. The special cells in the skin which give rise to colour in fishes are of two kinds—chromatophores which contain pigment granules and iridocytes which contain reflecting materials which mirror colours outside the fish.

The lateral line which is seen either as a complete or incomplete line along the outside of the fish consists of a series of modified scales with a pore which connects to the lateral line canal underneath. The lateral line system enables the fish to detect vibrations in the water.

RESPIRATION

Fishes use the dissolved oxygen in water for their respiration. Water is taken in through the mouth and expelled through the opercular openings. The gills separate the mouth cavity from the opercular opening so that water passes through them. There are four gill arches on either side and a large number of gill filaments, each covered by a very thin highly vascular mucous membrane, on each arch. The flow of water through the gills is an extremely complex mechanism which allows oxygen from the water to be taken up by the blood and for carbon dioxide in the blood to be given up to the water.

EXCRETION AND OSMOTIC REGULATION

In freshwater fishes the concentration of salts in the fish is greater than in the surrounding water. Since the epithelia of the gills, mouth and intestine are permeable to water and simple salts, water diffuses into and salts diffuse out of the freshwater fish. If this process was not regulated the fish would swell and be killed. In order to

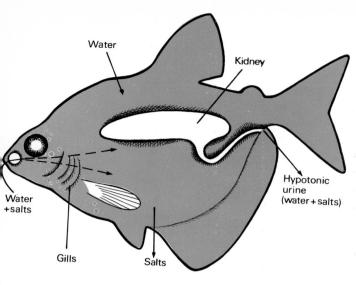

Movement of water and salts into and out of the body of a fish in fresh water

Internal features of a fish

expel this steady inflow of water the freshwater fish produces large amounts of dilute urine, while the kidney also excretes some nitrogenous waste products and small amounts of salts.

Salt loss, particularly of chlorides, also occurs through the gills and mouth epithelia but to compensate for this there are special cells in these sites which absorb chlorides and other salts selectively and this active absorption can considerably exceed the loss by osmosis.

SWIM BLADDER

The density of a fish is considerably greater than fresh water and this means that it would sink or have to be swimming constantly to maintain its position. If the fish can achieve neutral buoyancy by bringing its density nearer to that of fresh water it will have considerable advantages. Many fishes have accomplished this by the development of a gas bladder. This organ, which can easily be seen in many characins, enables the fish to hover more easily in mid-water and to rest in mid-stream with a minimum of effort, at the same time considerably reducing its energy requirements when swimming. Malfunction of this organ occasionally occurs for some unknown reason and causes abnormal postures and positioning of the fish.

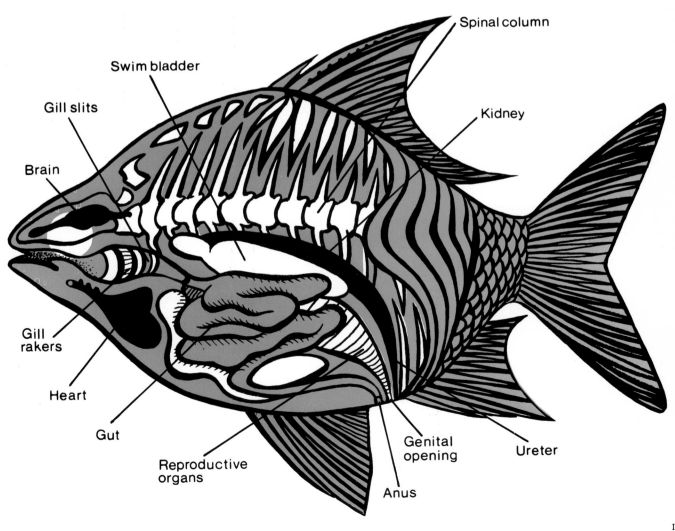

BREEDING FRESHWATER FISHES

One of the great attractions of keeping tropical freshwater fishes is that many of them will breed very easily in the aquarium provided that they are given the right conditions.

Most fishes are egg-layers, but there are a number of species which give birth to living young. In these fishes the male has an intromittent organ (gonopodium) by which internal fertilization of the female occurs, and the development of the embryo takes place in the ovary.

The egg-layers can be classified into the following five groups:

Egg-scatterers Fishes in this group, for example barbs and characins, scatter their eggs on the ground or among plants. The parental care of fish spawning in this manner is nil—they swim one way laying eggs and may swim back the other way eating them unless precautions are taken. In some of these groups the eggs are semi-adhesive and stick to plants or rocks.

Egg-placers These lay their eggs in neat clusters on rocks, plant pots or large-leafed plants. The cichlids usually spawn in this way. In many species of cichlid, such as the Jewel Fish (*Hemichromis bimaculatus*), the eggs are left to hatch where they are laid and then are taken to a depression in the gravel for the next few days. In other cichlids, as the Mozambique Cichlid (*Tilapia mossambica*), for example, the eggs are laid and fertilized and then taken into the mouth of one or other parent and incubated there. The fishes in this group are called mouth-brooders.

Nest-builders The most spectacular are the Anabantidae, many members of which build bubble nests, as the Siamese Fighting Fish (*Betta splendens*).

Egg-hangers These fishes lay their eggs, one or two at a time, on the roots of floating plants. Many species of killifishes, such as *Aphyosemion gardneri*, spawn in this way.

Egg-buryers These fishes bury their eggs in the mud or silt at the bottom of the pond, for example the egg-burying killifishes such as *Nothobranchius guentheri*.

GENERAL PRINCIPLES OF BREEDING

A good fish is good for two main reasons: it inherits good qualities from its parents, and secondly it has good environmental conditions, that is, it gets enough of the right foods, it has plenty of tank space, the water conditions are as congenial as possible, and so on.

Unfortunately, many species of tropical fishes are now said not to be as colourful as the same species were years ago. One reason for this is the relative ease of breeding freshwater fishes which encourages aquarists to breed unselectively from any poor fish to try and raise as many offspring as possible, many of them as bad as their parents. If we wish to improve our fishes we must breed with the best stock we can get and cull out any offspring which are less than perfect.

Siamese Fighting Fishes *(Betta splendens)* spawning below a bubble nest

Jewel Fish *(Hemichromis bimaculatus)* guarding eggs

Once a good stock for breeding has been obtained the fulfilment of the following principles leads to successful spawning:

1. Obtain a male and female, both of which should be mature. This seems obvious to everyone but in some species the sexes are so similar that most experienced aquarists will admit to having tried to breed two fishes of the same sex or with fishes too young to breed.

2. Condition the breeders, in separate tanks, for at least two weeks and feed them well with live foods.

3. Give the fishes correct water conditions, checking such points as the pH, hardness and any special requirements of individual species. Eggs of the Neon Tetra *(Hyphessobrycon innesi)*, for example, will not hatch in hard water and the eggs of the Madagascar Rainbow Fish *(Bedotia geayi)* will not hatch in soft water.

4. See that the temperature is correct; an increase in temperature of a few degrees is often a good stimulus to spawning.

5. Provide the proper spawning medium—peat fibre, floating plants, nylon wool mops, a plant pot, depending upon the spawning method of the fish.

6. Take care in raising the fry. This is very often the most difficult part of the whole breeding procedure, and feeding is particularly important.

As the fry get larger they should be moved into larger tanks for 'growing on' and they should be regularly inspected. All runts and fishes with abnormalities or with poor coloration should be removed and destroyed. Those which are growing particularly well and are the best in colour, shape and deportment should be earmarked for future breeding stock or for entering in breeders' classes in competitions.

GENETICS

The inheritance of various characteristics, such as shape, colour and finnage, obeys the same principles in tropical fishes as in all other creatures. Many of the characteristics are inherited in a dominant or recessive manner, obeying the laws of inheritance laid down by Mendel. It is not possible here to go into detail about the more complex principles of genetics but there is one important practical rule which will be of value to most fish keepers. If the hobbyist has a fish with a desired characteristic and as a result of crossing the fish this characteristic is not found among the offspring (that is, the characteristic is recessive) then the hobbyist can do two things to improve his chances of getting this characteristic back. He can cross the original parent, which has the desired characteristic, with one of its own offspring, when there is a fifty per cent chance of the young of this cross having the characteristic, or cross two of the offspring of the original mating together, when he will have a twenty-five per cent chance of getting youngsters with the desired feature.

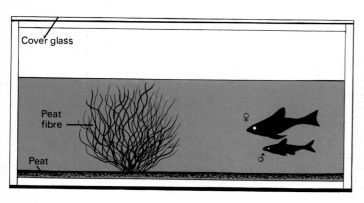

Breeding arrangement suitable for egg-scatterers such as characins

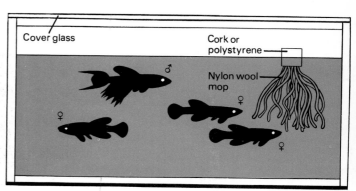

Breeding arrangement suitable for egg-hangers such as certain killifishes

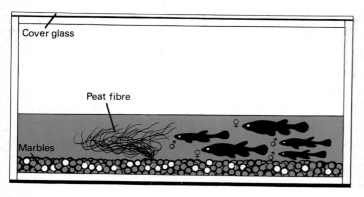

Breeding arrangement suitable for egg-scatterers such as barbs and danios

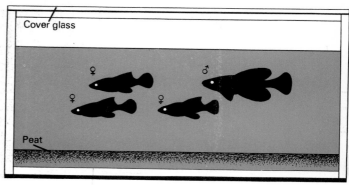

Breeding arrangement suitable for bottom-spawning killifishes

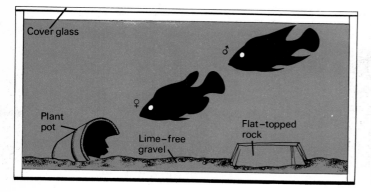

Breeding arrangement suitable for egg-placers such as cichlids

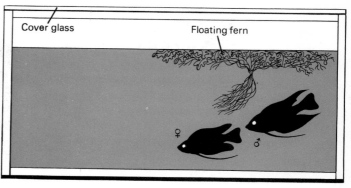

Breeding arrangement suitable for nest-builders such as anabantids

DISEASES OF FRESHWATER FISHES

There are a large number of diseases of fishes, many of which, happily, will never be seen by the aquarist. For many fish diseases neither cause nor cure is known, and the aquarist is warned that it is easy to spend more money buying cures for a fish than the fish is worth and that after some 'cures' the fish is worse off than before the treatment.

The classification of disease in fishes falls into two groups: congenital and acquired.

CONGENITAL DISEASES

These are diseases with which a fish is born, some of them being genetic in origin—missing gill plates and fins, for example—and are capable of being transmitted to its offspring; others are due to environmental influences during the incubation period of the egg.

ACQUIRED DISEASES

Trauma Fishes can be seriously injured by other fishes or by rough handling when netted. Excessive heat or cold can also damage or kill a fish, and water conditions are very important; excessive acidity or alkalinity or rapid changes in water conditions can make fishes ill or kill them.

Infections These are very important in the fish tank as the disease can spread and every fish in the tank become infected. Many infections with viruses or bacteria are not recognized but two protozoal infections—White Spot and Velvet disease—are very characteristic and very common.

WHITE SPOT DISEASE is an infection with *Ichthyophthirius multifilius* and the disease is always transmitted from an infected fish or an infected piece of equipment. Diagnosis is difficult in the early stages when the infected fish may have only one white spot, but such a fish can transmit the disease to every other fish in the tank. The white spot is a cystic stage of the parasite and on maturity it leaves the host and falls to the bottom of the tank. Multiplication takes place within this cyst and after a few days many daughter cells are present. The cyst then bursts, freeing the daughter cells which are free living and each seeks a new host and then burrows under its skin, feeding off the skin and mucus. When mature the parasite forms a cyst and the cycle is repeated. Once the White Spot parasite has left a fish it must find a new host within seven days or it will die.

The infected fish appears to have an itch and scratches against rocks. Then the white pin-point spots gradually develop; these are very few at first and are often seen best in the fins. If untreated they become very numerous and can kill the fish. Raise the temperature to 82°F (27°C); this speeds up the development of the cysts into the free-living form which can be easily killed as it is very susceptible to methylene blue. Add a sufficient quantity of one per cent solution of methylene blue to the water to make the tank a deep blue colour (about 1 ml/gallon repeated as colour fades until all spots are gone). Methylene blue kills many species of plants so put the fishes in an unplanted tank for this treatment. The planted tank with all its fishes removed should be left empty for two weeks, by which time any parasites will have died from the lack of a host.

VELVET is another infectious disease caused by a protozoan parasite. *Oodinium limneticum* attaches itself to a fish and sends rhizoids between the skin cells of its host through which it extracts tissue juices. The parasite grows for about seven days and can be seen as a pin-point golden spot. In mild infections, with just one or two parasites, it is very easily overlooked. The parasite matures, withdraws its rhizoids, drops off and forms a cyst within which the parasite divides producing 256 daughter cells. These then mature and escape from the cyst and are free swimming by means of two flagellae. Each 'swarmer' then swims about until it finds a fish—it can encyst again if it does not find one, probably remaining viable for some time. This parasite contains chlorophyl and can probably live a short time in well-lit tanks without a host.

Very often fishes do not appear ill until the infection is very heavy. The parasites are seen on dark-coloured fishes as yellowish in colour, 'dusted with sulphur', but in brightly coloured fishes they appear white. This parasite can kill; particularly heavy losses are caused in young fry. A one per cent solution of methylene blue (about 2 ml/gallon repeated as colour fades) kills the 'swarmer' stage of the parasite. At higher temperatures the life cycle is speeded up so raise the temperature to 80°F (27°C). Good proprietary cures are also available.

Cherry Barb suffering from White Spot Disease. Note the characteristic pin-point white spots seen most easily on the fins.

ICHTHYOPHONUS is a most important fungal disease of fishes and one which is not usually diagnosed by the aquarist. The fish is infected by feeding on contaminated material (infected fishes and perhaps infected *Cyclops*). From the gut the fungus can spread to any organ in the body; if the brain is infected the fish looses equilibrium, has protruding eyes and staggering movements; if the skin is infected ulcers develop on its surface.

Isolate the fishes for four days in a tank to which a one per cent solution of phenoxethol has been added (40–50 ml/gallon). For internal infections soak their food in the phenoxethol solution.

CANCERS All fishes can develop cancers, particularly as they become old. Some of the coloured fishes such as Siamese Fighters (*Betta splendens*) may develop pigmented tumours. No treatment is satisfactory.

VASCULAR LESIONS As fishes grow older they develop defects in blood vessels which can lead to sudden inexplicable deaths. There is no cure.

DEGENERATIVE DISEASES Some species are very prone to develop wasting diseases or skeletal deformities with age. Again, there is no cure.

It cannot be stressed too often that prevention is better than cure. Follow these simple rules:

1. Always buy healthy fishes. Examine them carefully and avoid all fishes with obvious disease such as Velvet or fishes with gill plates missing or which look ill at ease. Never buy fishes from a tank in which there are dead occupants or fishes suffering from one of the infectious diseases.

2. Isolate the newly bought fish in a separate tank for one month and keep separate equipment for this tank. At the end of one month's quarantine, examine the fish carefully in a good light to exclude Velvet and White Spot before placing it among other fishes.

The aquarist who has only one tank and cannot quarantine his new fish must be even more particular and careful when buying new stock. For further information on fish diseases see C. Van Duijn, *Diseases of Fish*, 2nd edition, London, Iliffe Book Ltd., 1967.

CATALOGUE OF FISHES

LIVE-BEARERS

Classification There are differences of opinion among taxonomists about whether the live-bearing tooth carps and the egg-laying tooth carps should belong to the same family as they have many features in common, but since from the hobbyist's point of view the method of reproduction is so important, they will be considered here as belonging to separate families. The live-bearing tooth carps can in this view be divided into four separate families: the Poeciliidae, containing such aquarium favourites as the Guppy (*Poecilia reticulata*), the Mollies (*Poecilia* species), the Platy (*Xiphophorus maculatus*), the Swordtail (*X. helleri*) and the Mosquito Fish (*Heterandria*

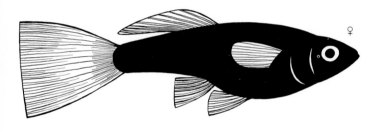

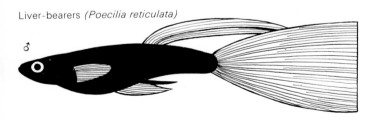

Liver-bearers (*Poecilia reticulata*)

formosa); and three other families of egg-laying tooth-carps—the Goodeidae, the Jenynsiidae and the Anablepidae—which contain some interesting fishes but which are rarely seen in the home aquarium.

There is one other fish with a live-bearing method of reproduction which is kept by some enthusiasts, the Halfbeak (*Dermogenys pusillus*); this is not a live-bearing tooth carp and belongs to a completely separate family, the Hemiramphidae.

Distribution and habitat The live-bearing tooth carps, of which there are about thirty genera, all come

from the New World. They are found as far north as the Great Lakes, through Latin America and the Caribbean islands, right down to the Argentine in the south. Obviously so many different genera distributed so widely have very differing habitats. Weed-ridden stagnant ponds with shallow water are a common type of habitat. Some species live in streams, some in lakes and some in rivers, including brackish waters at river mouths.

Most of these fishes will eat any kind of food but in their natural habitat mosquito larvae are preferred. Some species also eat algae and plant food. Many of the egg-laying tooth carps, and particularly the Guppy and *Gambusia* species, have been introduced into southern Europe and tropical areas of the world to help in mosquito control. Laboratory experiments have shown that an adult female Guppy will eat 123 and a male 13·4 mosquito larvae per day.

Method of reproduction Mature male fishes are easily recognized because they have a modification of the anal fin into a gonopodium. The gonopodium normally projects backwards but during mating it is twisted forwards and sideways and the tip inserted into the vent of the female. At this stage the male ejects the sperms, which travel along a groove in the gonopodium, enter the female and travel up the oviduct to the ovary where the eggs are fertilized. The eggs now develop, living on their own yolk; there is no nourishment obtained from the mother as in the placental animals. The embryos take thirty to forty days to develop and the young, which are $\frac{1}{2}$ in (1 cm) long, are fully formed at birth. They are usually born tail first and then swim to the surface to fill their air bladders. They begin immediately to search for food. The female fish is capable of storing sperm in her oviduct and one mating can produce a number of broods without any further fertilization by a male.

Breeding in the aquarium Select the male and female with the qualities of colour and finnage required. If seriously line breeding live-bearers it is also essential to have a virgin female, to rule out the possibility of a pregnancy resulting from stored sperm. Place both male and female inside a plastic net breeding trap ($12 \times 8 \times 8$ in with a $\frac{1}{4}$ in mesh; $30 \times 20 \times 20$ cm with a 6 mm mesh) and put this inside an $18 \times 10 \times 10$ in ($45 \times 25 \times 25$ cm) tank, positioned in the water so that $1\frac{1}{2}$ in (3 cm) of the

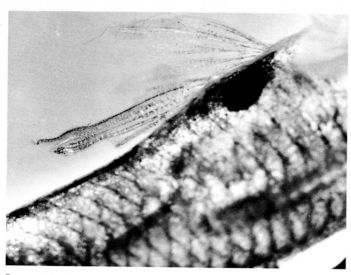
Gonopodium of male Guppy

trap projects above the water surface. I make the breeding trap from a sheet of garden plastic net bent into shape and sew up the sides with nylon fishing line. Some fishes such as *Heterandria formosa*, for example, need a net with a smaller mesh. Leave the parents together for a few days, although the male can be removed earlier if he is driving the female too hard. With mature fishes in good condition mating occurs within the first few hours. Leave the female on her own in the breeding trap and be careful not to overfeed as food drops through the bottom of the trap and goes bad if not removed. The female becomes very distended and drops the young after thirty to forty days' incubation (the earlier time at higher temperatures) and the fry swim through the mesh of the net and are thus not eaten by their mother. The female and the trap are removed when she looks thin and has obviously deposited all her brood. First spawnings are often small but with later spawnings up to 100 may be delivered. Feed the young on Brine Shrimp, Microworms and egg yolk emulsion, and as they grow increase the size and variety of their foods with such items as *Daphnia*, *Cyclops*, chopped Whiteworm and *Tubifex*, and minced liver. The better the feeding the quicker they grow. As soon as the fishes are large enough to be sexed, separate the males from the females, unless you wish random breeding among the offspring to take place. Any aquarist seriously breeding live-bearers must keep detailed notes of the crosses he has made as well as rigorously separating males and females and culling out poor specimens.

GUPPY *Poecilia reticulata* (*Lebistes reticulatus*)
Male grows to 1¼ in (3 cm), female to 2¼ in (5·5 cm);
   Venezuela, Trinidad and Barbados
This most common of aquarium fishes has now been introduced into most of the tropical areas of the world because of its use in mosquito control. The wild Guppy is very different from the good aquarium-bred fish; the male is smaller, basically grey with a few patches of black or colour on body or tail and with short fins and tail, while the female is a dull grey. By the efforts of

specialist breeders and the specialist Guppy societies many highly coloured and beautiful strains have been developed. Females now have colour in their fins. The specialist Guppy societies have introduced standards and a large number of varieties are recognized on the basis of their finnage shape or colour or a combination of these. Some of the finnage shapes which have been developed—so far in the males only—are:
FANTAIL—the tail spreads out like a fan.
VEILTAIL—the tail is long, widening moderately the further it gets from the caudal peduncle.
FLAGTAIL—the tail is as long as the body but very little wider than the caudal peduncle.
PINTAIL—the tail is round with a large dagger-like point.
SPEARTAIL—this is similar to the pintail but the point is not as exaggerated.
ROUNDTAIL—the tail fin is rounded.
SPADE TAIL—the tail is spade-shaped.
SWORDTAIL VARIETIES—Top sword: the upper lobe of the caudal fin is extended beyond the rest of the tail;
   Bottom sword: the extension this time is at the bottom of the tail fin;
   Double sword: the male has both a top and a bottom sword.
LYRETAIL—the tail fin is shaped like a lyre.

In combination with the pattern in the tail fin there are appropriate standards for the dorsal fin.

The following colour varieties have also been developed:
GOLDEN GUPPY—the fish is a buttercup-yellow in colour. This is a pure recessive form.
GOLDEN LACETAIL—the male and female are yellow in colour and the male has a lace pattern on the tail.
GREEN LACETAIL—the male has a green lace pattern on body and tail.

The mollies There has been a recent change in the scientific name of the mollies from the genus *Mollienesia* to the genus *Poecilia* and this is now widely accepted. Of the nine species of molly which are known to aquarium keepers only five species are commonly kept.

Mollies which are not in good health develop a condition called 'the shimmys', a characteristic shaking movement with drooped fins. Do not buy mollies with the shimmys but if your mollies should develop it increase the temperature of their water; make sure they have green food in their diet and plants in their aquarium and examine them carefully for evidence of diseases such as Whitespot or Velvet.

All pregnant mollies are prone to abort if placed in breeding traps when pregnant but if given a well-planted tank and good food they do not eat too many of their young. Sea salt—one teaspoon to ten litres of aquarium water—usually improves the water conditions for these fishes.

SHORT-FINNED MOLLY *Poecilia sphenops*
Male grows to 3½ in (9 cm), female to 4½ in (11·5 cm);
   central and northern South America
This species is found in both fresh and brackish water. Mollies are not the easiest of fish to keep but *P. sphenops*

Lyre-tailed Black Mollies *(Poecilia sphenops)*

is the hardiest of the commonly kept species. There are a number of colour varieties, the black one (the Black Molly) being the most popular. Other varieties are mottled black with an orange tail or grey-green with an orange tail. Varieties with lyre-tail caudal fins and curved dorsal fins have become increasingly popular in recent years.

SAIL-FIN MOLLY *Poecilia latipinna*
Grows to 3½–4 in (9–10 cm); southern United States
This fish comes from the coastal and estuarine regions of the United States from Carolina southwards into Central America as far as Yucatan. The chief characteristic of this species is the large dorsal fin of the male which starts just behind the gill cover and goes down most of the back. The female has a smaller dorsal fin. There are a number of colour varieties, the commonest being olive-green with five to six longitudinal bands of green, blue and red spots. The female is much duller than the male. The more

prized and much rarer colour variety is the Black Sail-fin Molly with yellow eyes and an orange-red edge to the sail fin. The best fishes of this variety come from large open pools from fish farms in the USA. This species matures late, at fifteen months, and lives for about three years.

GIANT SAIL-FIN MOLLY *Poecilia velifera*
Grows to 6 in (15 cm); Yucatan
This species is smaller in the aquarium. In the wild it is found in estuarine waters and, therefore, does better in hard alkaline water to which sea salt has been added. It is very similar to *P. latipinna* but grows bigger and has a larger dorsal fin with a higher fin ray count. There are a number of colour varieties but black varieties are not common.

DWARF TOP MINNOW, MOSQUITO FISH
Heterandria formosa
Male grows to ¾ in (2 cm), female to 1⅜ in (3.5 cm);
   North Carolina and Florida
This fish, which is the smallest of the live-bearers, is

Right Guppies *(Poecilia reticulata)* — the more brightly coloured fishes are male.

Below Swordtail *(Xiphophorus helleri)* male of Tuxedo Lyre-tailed variety displaying to Red Lyre-tailed female

Left Platy *(Xiphophorus maculatus)*

Below Halfbeak *(Dermogenys pusillus)*

yellowish-brown in colour with a broad dark band from nose to tail crossed by eight to twelve irregular dark bars.

These fishes are mature sexually at what seems to be a minute size. The eggs, once fertilized, do not all develop synchronously but at different rates so that the brood is born over about twelve days, a few each day. In spite of what many other breeders of this species report I have always found that the parents are likely to eat some of their young, so I keep the adults in a breeding trap with a mesh of $\frac{3}{16}$ in (4 mm) all the time, with plenty of floating plants so that the fry can thus easily escape.

SWORDTAIL *Xiphophorus helleri*
Male, without sword, grows to $3\frac{1}{2}$ in (9 cm), female to $4\frac{3}{4}$ in (12 cm); Mexico and Guatemala

This is a most interesting fish, especially at the present time when, by selective breeding and careful selection of new mutant strains by professional fish breeders in the USA, many new and interesting varieties are being introduced for the hobbyist to perfect. The size of swordtails today is much smaller than it was twenty years ago when swordtails 8 in (20 cm) long were exhibited at fish shows. The male swordtail has a prolongation of the lower rays of his caudal fin which forms the sword. Larger adult swordtails can be pugnacious and bully other fishes in the community tank.

The males are very ardent and courtship behaviour is most interesting to watch. I breed swordtails using the breeding trap method. Culling of weak fishes or those with undesirable characteristics is essential as is the separation of the sexes as soon as they can be distinguished.

The following varieties exist:
GREEN SWORDTAIL—this is the basic fish, yellowish-green in colour with a red zigzag line from behind the eye to the root of the tail.
RED SWORDTAIL—this is a deep red fish with a black-edged red sword.
RED-EYED RED SWORDTAIL—unfortunately, this variety is not common as the females seem to drop only a small number of young. It has a deep red body and fins, and red eyes.
ALBINO SWORDTAIL—this is a white fish with pink eyes, the longitudinal line being pink in colour.
BLACK SWORDTAIL—there are a number of varieties, the best completely black, but there are some attractive half red, half black strains.
WAGTAIL SWORDTAIL—the fins and lips are black; the body is red in the Red Wagtail Swordtail, or green in the Green Wagtail Swordtail.
FINS—the development of a top sword in some varieties has led to a lyre tail, a smaller variety of which is also found in females of this strain. This has been combined with the black fins of the Wagtail Swordtail. Another interesting development in recent years is the large flowing dorsal, the hi-fin dorsal which is extremely attractive.

PLATY *Xiphophorus maculatus*
Male grows to $1\frac{3}{4}$ in (4·5 cm), female to $2\frac{1}{2}$ in (6·5 cm); Mexico and Guatemala
This fish is a very close relative of the Swordtail, but is

deeper bodied, hardier and more peaceful. The wild fish is poorly coloured and although checked and red forms do occur in nature, there are many more colour varieties which have been developed by man. These include the following:
RED PLATY—this fish has a red body and fins.
YELLOW PLATY—the body and fins are yellow.
RED WAGTAIL and YELLOW WAGTAIL PLATIES—the tail fin and other fins are black but the body is red or yellow respectively.
MOON PLATY—this variety was an early development; the body is yellow with a black crescent moon at the root of the tail.
RED TUXEDO and GREEN TUXEDO PLATIES—these have the lower half of the body black with the upper half red or green respectively.

PLATY VARIATUS, VARIEGATED PLATY
Xiphophorus variatus
Male grows to 2 in (5 cm), female to 3 in (7·5 cm); southern Mexico

This species breeds easily with the Swordtail and the Platy. There are numerous colour varieties, the male usually being brighter than the female. A common variety is yellowish-brown in colour with black and blue spots on the body and a yellow dorsal fin. A recent development has been the introduction of the long flowing hi-fin.

Use a breeding trap to protect the young from the female. The fry are olive-green to brown when first born and develop their adult coloration slowly—it may be one year before colour is fully developed.

HALFBEAK *Dermogenys pusillus*
Male grows to $2\frac{1}{2}$ in (6·5 cm), female to $2\frac{3}{4}$ in (7 cm); Malay Peninsula

This species is not a live-bearing tooth carp. It has a characteristic elongated lower jaw. It is not a colourful fish, but it is very lively and lives just under the water surface. The males fight just like the male Siamese Fighting Fish (*Betta splendens*).

The incubation period for the internally hatched eggs is about eight weeks and twelve to twenty young fishes are delivered. This species is difficult to keep and, owing to a tendency in the females to produce stillborn young, difficult to breed.

CICHLIDS
Distribution and habitat This family of fishes comes from the southern United States, Central and South America, and Africa, and just two species suitable for the aquarium from Ceylon and India. They live in lakes and sluggish waters.

They exhibit complex territorial behaviour and have a tendency to be quarrelsome; some are extremely aggressive. Many species dig among the aquarium gravel, excavating pits, uprooting and maybe destroying plants. To offset these adverse family characteristics they are very beautiful fishes with highly developed parental instincts. Some species are excellent parents and their care of the young is delightful to watch.

A number of cichlid species, particularly *Tilapia* species, are being used to supplement the protein in the diet in many tropical areas of the world. The fishes are put as fingerlings into rice paddies when the rice is planted. They grow well and are harvested at a length of 4–5 in (10–12 cm) with the rice.

Method of reproduction Sexing is often difficult in this family and, as the fishes prefer to choose their own mates, it is a good idea to buy six to eight young, grow them up together and allow them to make their own selection. Mate selection can in some species be a rough business and 'trials of strength' with interlocking of jaws and butting take place. Sometimes an unacceptable female may have to be removed for her own safety.

Cichlids (male *Pelmatochromis pulcher*; female *P. subocellatus*)

During courtship both fishes colour up and in some species the female can be more colourful than the male, an uncommon occurrence in the fish world. The fishes clean a flat-topped rock, a broad leaf or a plant pot if they are given one, after which the female starts to lay, covering a few square inches of stone with neat rows of eggs which are then fertilized by the male. Some species prefer to dig a hole in the gravel in which they deposit their eggs.

When the eggs hatch they are often removed and put in a shallow pit dug in the gravel where they are fanned and fussed over for a few days by the parents until the fry are free swimming. The fry are then gathered into a tight shoal and taken for a swim by the proud parents. In some species, one parent takes the eggs into its mouth as soon as they are laid and the eggs are incubated (brooded) there until they hatch and the fry are free swimming. During this time the parent does not feed. The set up for the tank spawning of cichlids is shown on page 16.

It is customary to talk of two groups of cichlids which are classified by size: dwarf cichlids, which grow no longer than 4–5 in (10–12 cm), and which are generally peaceful and can be kept with communities of other fishes in tanks as small as $18 \times 10 \times 10$ in ($45 \times 25 \times 25$ cm), and the large cichlids which grow from 5–25 in (12·5–63·5 cm), even under aquarium conditions, and on the whole are aggressive and better kept on their own in large tanks. No special water conditions are necessary for keeping most cichlids.

Dwarf cichlids

Genus *APISTOGRAMMA* Fishes of this genus are small and do well in the aquarium. They prefer soft, acid water and are happier if provided with a few rocks and clumps of plants in which they can hide. They will live in small $18 \times 10 \times 10$ in ($45 \times 25 \times 25$ cm) tanks and are no problem in the community tank.

AGASSIZI DWARF CICHLID *Apistogramma agassizi*
Male grows to 3 in (7·5 cm), female to 3–4 in (8 cm);
Amazon Basin and Bolivia

This species is yellowish-brown in colour with a brown-black stripe from mouth to caudal fin. The adult fishes are very easy to sex, the female is smaller and has a rounded caudal fin whereas the male has a pointed caudal fin edged with blue.

Use the typical cichlid breeding set up with a plant pot. I usually find that if I remove the male, the female makes a good job of rearing the fry. First spawnings are often eaten—I suppose the mother is just a learner for she does not usually eat subsequent spawnings. I do not find artificial rearing a very successful method of breeding this species.

THE RAMIREZI or RAM CICHLID *Apistogramma ramirezi*
Grows to 2 in (5 cm); Venezuela

Although this species is an aquarium favourite it is not easy to keep or breed. I think of it as the Red Indian fish because the male has a very long extension of the second spine in the dorsal fin which is like a feather in the head-dress of a Red Indian. The basic colour is a pale crimson with a transverse line over the eye and a dark spot under the dorsal fin.

I use a different technique for breeding this fish. I select my pair for breeding and condition them separately, preparing a special breeding tank filled with soft acid water (less than 20 ppm and a *p*H between 5·5 and 6) into which a stone with a slightly concave surface is placed. Aerate the water for twenty-four hours at a temperature of 78°F (26°C). Do not use any gravel. The adults are put in the tank late at night and are not fed in the breeding tank; they usually spawn within two days and are removed and reconditioned if they do not spawn before.

Once the eggs are laid I remove the parents, add two drops of a one per cent solution of methylene blue to the water (this just colours the water very faintly) and put an air stone below the eggs to maintain a brisk supply of air bubbles to fan them. These eggs seem very susceptible to dirt and bacteria. The fry hatch in two days and become free swimming in another five when they should be given a feed of newly hatched Brine Shrimp. Even at this stage bacteria or low oxygen tension produced by feeding egg yolk or infusoria kills the fry.

Oscar or Velvet Cichlid *(Astronotus ocellatus)*

Genus *NANNACARA*
GOLDEN-EYED DWARF CICHLID *Nannacara anomala*
Grows to 3 in (7·5 cm); western Guianas

This is a peaceful and hardy species. The male is yellowish-brown with a black stripe from the eye to the caudal peduncle and a larger and more pointed dorsal fin than the duller-coloured female. The intensity of coloration of these fishes changes very frequently but becomes very much more brilliant at spawning time.

They spawn in the typical cichlid manner on a stone or flowerpot, after which the female only looks after the eggs. The fry hatch after forty-eight hours and are taken and put into a shallow depression dug in the gravel by the female. After about five days they become free swimming.

Genus *PELMATOCHROMIS* There are seven species in this genus known to aquarists but only one has become really popular.

PELMATOCHROMIS KRIBENSIS
Male grows to 4 in (10 cm), female to 3 in (7·5 cm); Niger delta

Both sexes are equally colourful; the male is recognized by the presence of black spots (about five in number) on the upper aspect of the caudal fin, and the female in breeding condition has a bright reddish-purple abdomen. This species is the great digger of the aquarium— it can dig a hole 3 in (7·5 cm) in diameter down to the bottom glass of the aquarium in a few hours and fill it up in even less time.

These fishes spawn best in soft acid water which must therefore be provided for them together with lime-free gravel. I use a plant pot for them to spawn on and condition the pair separately before putting them in the breeding tank. Courtship can last for days before they eventually spawn. The young hatch in three days and are then kept in a depression in the gravel for another three days before they become free swimming. My experience of these fishes is that each spawning has turned out to be either predominantly male or predominantly female. Broods are usually small, under forty.

Large cichlids from South America
OSCAR, MARBLED, PEACOCK or VELVET CICHLID *Astronotus ocellatus*
Grows to 13 in (33 cm); Venezuela to Paraguay

If well-fed this fish grows remarkably quickly, a gentle giant which will, however, eat most fishes considerably smaller than itself. Adults are a greyish-green with black patches and red circular markings. Young fishes have a much more definite variable pattern than the adult. The adult male is usually slimmer than the female and generally has three spots at the base of the dorsal fin.

Breed at 4–5 in (10–12 cm) in the usual cichlid fashion.

Genus *AEQUIDENS* There are six species of this genus which are known to aquarists, including fairly popular species such as the Keyhole Cichlid (*A. maroni*) and the Black Acara (*A. portalegrensis*). My favourite fish in this

Angelfish *(Pterophyllum* sp.)

Above Jewel Fishes *(Hemichromis bimaculatus)* guarding fry

Left Discus *(Symphysodon* sp.) with young

genus is the Blue Acara (*A. pulcher*) which is a typical member of the genus.

BLUE ACARA *Aequidens pulcher*
Grows to 7 in (18 cm); Trinidad and Venezuela
The best specimens are often seen in the large tanks of public aquaria, the males distinguished by their large and more pointed dorsal and anal fins. The basic body colour is a yellowish-green with eight irregular dark transverse bands over the sides and many green spots and wavy lines on the body and head.

It breeds in the normal cichlid manner, and although the courtship is boisterous parental care is good. It digs a lot and uproots plants.

Genus *CICHLOSOMA* Over twenty species of this genus have been kept by aquarists; it includes relatively peaceful fishes such as the Barred or Flag Cichlid (*Cichlosoma festivum*) and the Firemouth Cichlid (*C. meeki*), as well as the more aggressive Jack Dempsey (*C. biocellatum*) and the very beautiful but highly aggressive Texas Cichlid (*C. cyanoguttatum*). A number of species new to aquarists such as the Red Devil (*C. erythraeum*), for example, have been imported in recent years.

FIREMOUTH CICHLID *Cichlosoma meeki*
Grows to 6 in (15 cm); Yucatan and Guatemala
This species is characterized by the bright red throat and jaw, but the male has brighter colours and more pointed

Discus *(Symphysodon* sp.)

Golden Lake Nyasa Cichlid *(Pseudotropheus auratus)*

Mozambique Cichlid (*Tilapia mossambica*)

and extended dorsal and anal fins. On the whole, this fish is well behaved; it is even possible to keep adults in a community tank, although they tend to do some excavating and to appropriate three quarters of the tank space as their own territory when spawning. They are good parents.

Genus *PTEROPHYLLUM* There are three species of angelfishes, *Pterophyllum altum*, *P. eimekei* and *P. scalare*, which interbreed so that many specimens are intermediate forms between the three. Sterba (*Freshwater Fishes of the World*, London, 1962) says that pure lines of angelfishes are rarely found in captivity. They are native to the Orinoco and Amazon Basins, growing up to 6 in (15 cm) long and 8 in (20 cm) deep. They are best kept in tanks well-planted with *Echinodorus* and *Cryptocoryne* species.

Angelfishes are difficult to sex so it is better to buy six to eight young fishes, grow them up and let them choose their own mates. When a pair begins an obvious courtship remove all the other fishes and incline a length of slate, vermiculite or plastic about $2\frac{1}{2} \times 8$ in (6×20 cm) in size in one corner of the tank for them to spawn on. The eggs, up to 1,000 in number, are laid in neat rows on this. Most breeders of angels remove the slate once the eggs have been laid and raise the eggs artificially. This usually results in better yields than when the parents are allowed to raise the young.

Put the slate in a small bare tank with similar water to that in which the fishes spawned, adding one to two drops only of a one per cent solution of methylene blue. Put an airstone in such a position that the bubbles cause a current which constantly bathes the eggs. The young hatch in twenty-four to thirty-six hours and at first hang on to the slate by means of a small thread. Some hours later they fall off the slate and collect in 'balls' on the bare bottom of the tank. Keep the aerator going until the fry become free swimming four to five days later. They should now be fed on newly hatched Brine Shrimp and Micro-worm. Young angels are not angel-shaped but gradually achieve the 'proper' shape as they get older. As they grow, cull out all runts, those with de-

fective gill plates or missing fins, and only raise the best fishes.

There are now three colour varieties as well as the ordinary angel: the Black Angel, the Black Lace and the Marbled Angelfish. A variety with long flowing fins, the Veiltail, has been produced in recent years.

DISCUS, POMPADOUR FISH *Symphysodon* species
Grows to 6 in (15 cm) long and 8 in (20 cm) deep; Amazon and its tributaries
These fishes have been classified by Schultz (*Tropical Fish Hobbyist*, June, 1960) as follows:
Symphysodon aequifasciata aequifasciata (Green Discus)
S. a. axelrodi (Brown Discus)
S. a. haraldi (Blue Discus)
S. discus (Red Discus, the Heckel)
There appears also to be another colour variety of this fish—the Green Heckel.

These are beautiful saucer-shaped fishes but difficult to keep and even more difficult to breed. They are very variable in colour, which changes with changes in their environment. The basic body colours vary from brown to orange-red and deep blue. They have a number of dark vertical stripes and an irregular pattern of blue lines on the head and body. In my experience fishes 3 in (7.5 cm) deep are much more likely to survive than those with a body depth of 1 in (2.5 cm). They need an acid pH (between 6.2 and 6.6) and soft water (under 80 ppm). Soft water can be acidified to the desired pH by using a peat filter as described on page 7. Use a lime-free gravel and plant patches of the tank with *Echinodorus* species, using floating plants to reduce the light intensity. The temperature should be 75–85°F (24–29°C).

Softer water (down to 10 ppm) and a lower pH (down to pH 5) are recommended for successful spawning. The fishes lay their eggs on the glass or on a plant leaf and both parents look after and fan the eggs, which hatch after about four days.

The fry are free swimming at the end of a week and feed off a special secretion from the skin of both parents for about thirty days. This secretion, 'cichlid milk', seems to be essential for the nutrition of the fry and they die if their parents are removed. When about two weeks old, the fry begin to take Brine Shrimps and other foods can be introduced gradually. The best account of breeding the Discus is by Roy and Gwen Skipper, *Pompadours successfully bred in Britain*, in *Water Life*, June–July, 1956. This was followed up by further articles in the issues of this journal for December, 1956 and April–May, 1957.

Large cichlids from Asia These are represented in the aquarium by *Etroplus maculatus* (Orange Chromide) and *E. surratensis* (Green Chromide), the former coming from fresh and brackish water in India and Ceylon, and the latter from brackish water off Ceylon. The Orange Chromide needs a temperature of 78°F (26°C) for breeding and lays its eggs on the rockwork. Both parents take care of the fry. The Green Chromide only does well if kept in a mixture of one part of salt water to four parts of fresh water at 78°F (26°C).

Large African cichlids There are a large number of cichlids which come from Africa.

EGYPTIAN MOUTH-BROODER *Haplochromis multicolor*
Grows to $3\frac{1}{2}$ in (9 cm); East Africa and the lower Nile
These are peaceful fishes which in breeding condition are very attractive. The body is a pale rust colour but has green and golden highlights and the fins are bright rust-red with green rays.

They spawn in depressions which they dig in the gravel and immediately the female picks up the eggs in her mouth where they are incubated for about ten days. She then releases the fry but takes them into the mouth again at times of danger and at night for about another ten days. The female does not feed during the time the eggs are incubating.

THE JEWEL FISH *Hemichromis bimaculatus*
Grows to 6 in (15 cm); Congo, Niger and Nile
A popular species, these fishes do not cause too much trouble if in a tank by themselves, but the male may kill the female if she is not ready to spawn when he is. They spawn on a flat stone after both fishes have cleaned it very thoroughly. The eggs are neatly laid $\frac{1}{8}$ in (3 mm) apart over an area 2–3 in (5–7.5 cm) in diameter.

Both parents carefully fan and clean the eggs over the next two days until the fry hatch. The young are then taken to a pit dug in the gravel and again beautifully cared for by both parents working a 'shift system'. The fry are moved two or three times to newly dug depressions until they are free swimming five days later. The fry can be left with the parents until the parents show signs of spawning again.

MOZAMBIQUE CICHLID *Tilapia mossambica*
Grows to 15 in (38 cm); East Africa
This fish belongs to a genus containing many large fishes which are eaten as food. *Tilapia mossambica* has been taken all over the tropics for this purpose and occasionally re-appears with an exotic common name; for example, a few years ago it became popular in England as the Hawaiian Mouth-brooder.

There are both grey and black colour varieties of this fish. Aquarium specimens rarely grow more than 6 in (15 cm) long but breed when they are as small as 4 in (10 cm). The female mouth-broods the eggs for about ten days.

The Lake Nyasa cichlids These are a group of cichlids from a number of different genera which come from Lake Nyasa in Africa. The water in the lake is hard and alkaline and in order to keep these fishes these conditions must be reproduced in the tank; the water must be hard (200 ppm) and alkaline (pH 7·5–8). Most of them are adapted to eating algae as well as live foods and will also eat plants, so should be given vegetable foods such as chopped spinach and lettuce in the aquarium. They are very aggressive fishes and should not be kept with other species. If buying an adult pair of any of these fishes the female should be separated from the male by a glass partition in the aquarium until they settle down.

GOLDEN LAKE NYASA CICHLID *Pseudotropheus auratus*
Grows to 4 in (10 cm)
The male is golden in colour becoming dark blue with a yellow dorsal fin at breeding time; the female is yellow with two longitudinal dark stripes. There is another colour variety of this fish in which the male is bright blue at breeding time and the female white with black stripes.

My experience with this species is that the male is very aggressive towards the female, so she must be provided with plenty of hiding places. The male digs a pit in the gravel into which the female lays the eggs. When they have been fertilized by the male, she takes the eggs into her mouth and incubates them there. It is at this point that the male should be removed. The eggs are brooded for three to four weeks and the fry are $\frac{1}{4}$ in (6 mm) long when they are allowed to venture from the female's mouth.

ANABANTIDS (LABYRINTH FISHES)
This is one of the families of tropical fishes which breathe air. Most tropical fishes asphyxiate in water containing less than about 0·3 to 1·5 ml of oxygen per litre. In some tropical ponds and swamps which contain a large amount of decaying organic matter oxygen levels below 1 ml/litre are found an inch or two below the surface. Anabantids which live in such conditions have developed a method of breathing atmospheric air. They have a relatively large folded organ in a sac at the back of the gill chamber—the labyrinth organ. The surface of this organ is richly supplied with blood vessels which take up the atmospheric oxygen from the air. As a litre of air contains 200 mls of oxygen compared with the 8 ml of dissolved oxygen in a litre of well-oxygenated water, this is a very efficient method of respiration.

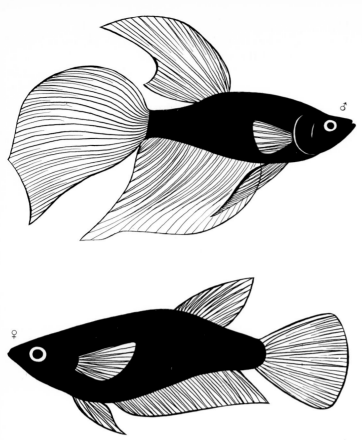

One member of the family, *Anabas testudineus* (Climbing Perch, Climbing Fish) which is widely distributed in the Far East, lives in swamps and is able to walk from one pond to the next, using its tail fin as the means of locomotion and its pectoral and pelvic fins as props. For these excursions it is dependent upon its labyrinth organ for respiration. An aggressive and unattractive fish, it is not very often seen in aquaria.

Distribution and habitat All the Anabantidae come from the Old World, from Asia—ranging from Korea in the north-east, through China, South-east Asia, India and Ceylon—and from Africa south of the Sahara. They live in flooded rice paddies, in drainage ditches, irrigation canals, streams and rivers. Many of the habitats are heavily planted and often have top (floating) plants. In the aquarium these fishes have no special demands, eating all dry foods and all live foods of suitable size. Water conditions can range from soft to hard without any apparent advantage or disadvantage to most species of Anabantidae. Temperatures of about 75°F (24°C) are suitable for the majority of species.

Method of reproduction Most of the members of this family are bubble nest breeders, some fishes such as *Betta splendens* (Siamese Fighting Fish) building a good nest, others such as *Colisa chuna* (Honey Gourami) building a very poor one.

The young hatch in thirty-six hours and become free swimming after another three to four days, at which time the male (who has been very busy replacing any falling fry) should be removed. Egg yolk emulsion for the first few weeks followed by newly hatched Brine Shrimp and Micro-worms is essential. The labyrinth

Above Anabantids *(Betta splendens)*

Below Male Siamese Fighting Fish *(Betta splendens)* building a bubble nest

organ is not present at birth but develops two to three weeks after the fry have hatched. Some species are mouth-brooders.

Genus *BETTA*   There are seven species of *Betta* which have been kept from time to time by hobbyists, but the only one commonly kept is *Betta splendens*.

SIAMESE FIGHTING FISH *Betta splendens*

Grows to 2½ in (6·5 cm); Thailand and Malay Peninsula
This fish lives in the flooded paddy fields, irrigation ditches, dirty streams and ponds of South-east Asia. The pugnacity of the males, which will fight each other until the fins of both are ripped to pieces, is responsible for their common name. In Thailand this fighting has led to public contests with bets being laid on the winner. A male with two or three females can be kept in the community tank though he will get his fins trimmed by fast-moving characins such as Serpae (*Hyphessobrycon callistus serpae*).

For breeding this species choose sexually mature adults, making sure that both a male and a female have been selected. The female should be well distended with ova; a reluctant female may be killed by the male. Set up the tanks as illustrated on page 16. A bare black-painted bottom to the tank enables the fishes to see the eggs easily rather than losing them among the gravel. The water depth should be about 10 in (25 cm) as too shallow a water depth does not allow the fishes sufficient distance for mating. Use either a piece of floating fern or an artificial floating plant—I use a thin piece of polystyrene 2 in (5 cm) in diameter with about six strands of nylon wool 3 in (7·5 cm) long as 'roots'. The temperature of the water should be 80°F (27°C).

Put the male in the tank and put the female in a jam jar suspended in the tank later in the evening. This stimulates both fishes and the male will often start to build his nest around the floating plant. Next morning gently tip out the female. The courtship is now fierce—the male first chases the female, extending all his fins and gill covers and then goes back and adds a few more bubbles to the nest. This is repeated and the female is gradually enticed under the nest. She too intensifies in colour and often shows transverse darker bands. Eventually the male wraps himself around the female, turning her over and at the same time squeezing and releasing his milt. At first only one or two eggs are released as the embracing pair float down towards the bottom from the nest. They break apart and the male picks up the eggs and blows them into the nest. The female swims under the nest and the embrace is repeated, each time more eggs being released. Some females seem to be much more cooperative than others.

Eventually the embrace yields no further eggs and at this point the male chases off the female. Gently remove her, taking care not to damage the nest. The male now looks after the eggs and nest, blowing more bubbles, picking up any fallen eggs and removing infertile ones as the need arises. The eggs hatch in thirty-six hours at 80°F (27°C) and the fry hang tail down from the nest. They can be easily seen at this stage. Some fall out of the

Male and female Siamese Fighting Fishes in courtship display

Kissing Gouramis *(Helostoma temmincki)*

nest and their swimming capacity is not sufficient for them to rise again to the surface but they are picked up by the male and blown back into the nest. About three to four days later the fry are free swimming and horizontal in the water. The male should now be removed; he has done his job.

The fry gradually swim away from the disintegrating nest and should be fed on hard boiled egg yolk squeezed between finger and thumb into the water or on commercial first foods for fry. About two to three weeks later introduce newly hatched Brine Shrimp and Micro-worms. Give other larger foods such as chopped White-worms as the fishes grow.

Genus *COLISA* All members of this genus have the pectoral fins modified into long 'feelers' which the fishes use as sense organs.

STRIPED or BANDED GOURAMI *Colisa fasciata*
Grows to 4¾ in (12 cm); India and South-east Asia
This fish has a basic body colour of rust-red with eight to ten diagonal light blue bars. Its other popular name —the Giant Gourami—would be better reserved for a much larger member of the Gourami family, *Osphronemus goramy*. This species is a typical bubble nest breeder.

THICK-LIPPED GOURAMI *Colisa labiosa*
Grows to 3 in (7·5 cm); Burma
This gourami is very easy to keep and does well in the community tank. It is brownish in colour with very irregular green-blue transverse bars on the body. This species is also a bubble nest blower, but the nest is a very poor one.

DWARF GOURAMI *Colisa lalia*
Grows to 2 in (5 cm); India
This is a small shy fish which prefers to live in well-planted tanks. It is easy to sex as the female is silvery compared to the beautiful male which is red with a large number of light blue bars on the body and rows of blue spots on the fins.

For breeding put the pair in a tank with no gravel, 4 in (10 cm) of water only and plenty of floating plants such as Indian Fern, Water Lettuce and Duckweed. The temperature should be about 80°F (27°C). The male blows the nest using bits of plants to reinforce it. The spawning act is similar to that of most bubble nest breeders and the parents should be removed after spawning has been completed.

The fry hatch in thirty-six hours and as they are extremely small can only take the finest foods. Green water which contains *Euglena* and *Chlamydomonas*, two small infusoria, is the ideal food. If not available add small amounts of egg yolk emulsion as soon as the fishes have spawned. This stimulates the growth of infusoria in the water and these are then ready for when the fry hatch. Growth is slow for about two to three weeks and over fifty per cent of the fry are lost. After this time the fry are large enough to take Brine Shrimp and Micro-worms and growth is faster.

When picking Dwarf Gouramies, either at the dealer's or when selecting the best from your own spawning, choose only those with unbroken matching diagonal bars and with deep bodies.

HONEY GOURAMI *Colisa chuna*
Grows to 2 in (5 cm); India
This is a shy fish in the community tank and only really at its best when sexually mature and in breeding condition. The body is orange-brown, darker on the ventral surface, and the dorsal fin is bright yellow.

For breeding use a 'bare bottom tank' with plenty of floating plants, a water depth of 4–8 in (10–20 cm) and a temperature of about 80°F (27°C). The nest built by the male is a very thin one but may cover the whole surface of an 18 × 10 × 10 in (45 × 25 × 25 cm) tank.

The fry hatch in twenty-four hours and are very black in colour. They are as small as Dwarf Gourami fry and need the same types of very small initial foods.

KISSING GOURAMI *Helostoma temmincki*
Grows to 12 in (30 cm) in the wild; South-east Asia
This species is an overall yellowish-pink in colour with black eyes and translucent fins. It is an aquarium favourite largely because of the 'kissing' behaviour which these fishes exhibit when two grasp each other with their turned back, extended lips. This apparently affectionate pattern of behaviour is probably a form of aggressive display.

This fish will eat a varied diet but must be given vegetable foods. It is reported that the eggs float to the surface by themselves and that the Kissing Gourami does not build a bubble nest.

GOURAMI *Osphronemus goramy*
Grows to 24 in (60 cm) long in the wild and 12 in (30 cm) deep; Sunda Islands
This species is now found all over South-east Asia as it has been widely distributed as a food fish. It is a dull brown in colour, darker on the head, with orange fins.

This is an omnivorous fish and should be given vegetable and flake foods. It builds a bubble nest and the male looks after the fry.

CHOCOLATE GOURAMI *Sphaerichthys osphronemoides*
Grows to 2½ in (6·5 cm); South-east Asia
The colour pattern of this species is variable but the basic body colour is a deep chocolate brown with four or five yellowish vertical lines. There is a vague yellowish line from the eye to the caudal peduncle. The females are fatter and deeper-bodied, while the males have a more pointed dorsal fin.

These fishes are difficult to establish. In my experience the most successful method is to keep them in soft acid water at a temperature of 78°F (26°C), with a few floating plants and a half-inch layer of previously boiled peat on the tank bottom (see page 00). I have never seen them eating algae or plant material but they eat all live foods with Whiteworms the firm favourite. All artificial foods are ignored.

They are said to be mouth-brooders.

Genus *TRICHOGASTER*
THE LEERI or PEARL GOURAMI *Trichogaster leeri*
Grows to 4½ in (11·5 cm); South-east Asia
This is a nice peaceful fish which does best of all in a well-planted tank. The whole fish is covered with pearl-coloured spots, the throat is bright red and there is a dark line from the mouth to the caudal peduncle. The male is thinner with more pointed fins, and he builds the large bubble nest and is responsible for the care of the eggs.

SNAKESKIN GOURAMI *Trichogaster pectoralis*
Grows to 10 in (25 cm); Thailand, Malaysia and Vietnam
This peaceful and hardy fish derives its common name from its coloration, irregular greenish or yellow lines on a general greenish background, which looks like snakeskin. It is a bubble nest breeder.

Right Siamese Fighting Fishes in courtship

Below Dwarf Gouramis *(Colisa lalia)*. The male — on the right — shows broken diagonal bars.

Opposite Chocolate Gourami *(Sphaerichthys osphronemoides)*

THREE-SPOT GOURAMI *Trichogaster trichopterus trichopterus*
Grows to 6 in (15 cm); South-east Asia
This is a very commonly kept fish. It is a dull mottled blue colour. The three spots from which it gets its popular name are the eye, the spot under the dorsal fin and the spot at the base of the tail.

Courtship often starts with a little playful butting. The male blows a good-sized nest and spawning takes place. The female should then be removed and the male also when the fry become free-swimming.

BLUE or OPALINE GOURAMI *Trichogaster trichopterus sumatranus*
Grows to 3 in (7·5 cm)
This fish is not known in the wild and is said to have originated in Sumatra as a cultivated species. It is a subspecies of *T. t. trichopterus* but much more blue in colour and without the spots. It breeds just as easily and as prolifically as the previous fish.

DWARF CROAKING GOURAMI *Trichopsis pumilus*
Grows to 1¾ in (4·5 cm); Vietnam, Thailand and Sumatra
This is one of the so-called 'croaking' gouramis although the noise produced by this fish is a gentle, rapid clicking and is only heard when the fish house is very quiet. It is similar in shape and colour to the Blue Gourami.

For breeding put this species in a tank without any gravel but with a few floating plants and a bunch of large-leafed plants such as Cryptocorynes, anchored down in one corner by a piece of glass. The male builds a small bubble nest under one of the plant leaves. Spawnings are small and the eggs hatch in thirty hours at 80°F (27°C). The parents do not seem to eat the fry but neither do they give them any care.

TALKING or CROAKING GOURAMI *Trichopsis vittatus*
Grows to 2½ in (6·5 cm); Thailand, Malaysia and Vietnam
This species is generally yellowish-brown in colour. It is a bubble nest breeder, and the same techniques should be used as for the previous species. Both sexes can make croaking noises.

Genus *MACROPODUS*
PARADISE FISH *Macropodus opercularis*
Grows to 3½ in (9 cm); China, Korea, Vietnam and Taiwan
This is a very attractive fish; one dominant coloured form is brown with blue-green vertical bars and there is also a recessive albino form which is pale pink with pink eyes. It is a very undemanding species and can be kept in temperatures as low as 60°F (15°C), although the temperature should be raised to 75°F (24°C) for breeding. It is aggressive both to other fishes and to other members of the same species. It is a typical bubble nest breeder.

Three-spot Gouramis *(Trichogaster trichopterus)*

Opposite Blue Gularis *(Aphyosemion sjoestedti)*

Above *Nothobranchius guentheri*

Genus *CTENOPOMA* Members of this genus come from Africa and are known as the African climbing perches, although they do no climbing or walking on the land. The body shape is more cichlid than anabantid and they are all predators, eating fishes and insect larvae. Some species are very leaf-shaped in appearance and even drift through the water like dead leaves.

THE KILLIFISHES

Classification The killifishes or egg-laying tooth carps are a large family closely related to the live-bearing

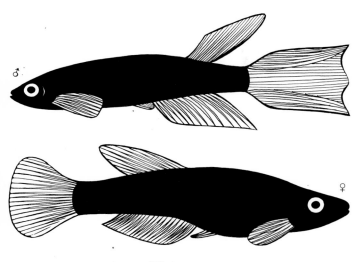

Killifishes *(Aphyosemion vexillifer)*

tooth carps. The killifishes are all egg-laying. Over 140 species are known and many fishes new to the aquarist are being imported thanks to the enthusiasm of members of the British and American Killifish Associations, societies devoted to keeping and breeding this family.

Distribution and habitat The members of this family are widely distributed; some are not strictly tropical as they come from areas outside the tropics—from the USA and Japan in the north to as far south as the Argentine. All these fishes live in ponds, swamps or streams. Some species live in areas where the wet and dry seasons are very distinct, the ponds or streams drying up completely during the dry season, but most species live in areas where the rainfall is more equable and there is plenty of water all the year round. Very often the water in which they live is soft and, because it contains much decaying vegetation, also acid. Owing to the surrounding vegetation the amount of sunlight falling on the water is small so that the pool is shaded and the temperature not very high.

If these fishes are given the correct conditions they are very easy to keep. The water should be soft and should be acidified, using peat as follows. Boil the peat for five minutes in soft water and allow it to cool. Then squeeze out the excess moisture from the peat and add enough to the aquarium to cover the bottom to a depth of $\frac{1}{2}$ in (13 mm). The peat will float for a day or two but then sinks to the bottom. Do not put any gravel in the tank since the calcium compounds present in most gravels will make the water hard. As plants cannot be rooted in peat these tanks cannot have bottom plants although floating plants such as Indian ferns, *Salvinia* and Duckweed are appreciated. The water temperature is best kept at 70–74°F (21–23°C). All killifishes are good jumpers so keep a well-fitting cover glass on the tanks and do not use a bright light.

Some killifishes, such as *Epiplatys*, *Pachypanchax* and

Gardneri *(Aphyosemion gardneri)*

Pachypanchax playfairi

Rivulus species, can be kept in the community tank, but *Aphyosemion*, *Nothobranchius* and *Cynolebias* species do not do well under community tank conditions. They all prefer live foods, but the members of the community tank group will take dried foods. In recent years these fishes have been used for malaria control purposes because of their fondness for mosquito larvae.

Method of reproduction These fishes are divided into two main groups, the egg-hangers and the egg-buryers.

The egg-hangers lay their eggs on the roots of floating plants and spawning takes place intermittently over a period of months, a few eggs being laid each day. The eggs take about two to three weeks to hatch depending upon the species and environmental factors, for example, temperature is most important. All egg-hangers live in equatorial rain forest conditions with a good rainfall all the year round.

The other group, the egg-buryers, live in savannah conditions where the water in which they live evaporates in the dry season. The adults die of asphyxia as the water disappears but their eggs, laid in the mud at the bottom of the pool, are prevented from drying out by the surrounding mud. When the rain comes three to four months later the eggs hatch in a few hours, the fry grow rapidly and are sexually mature within two months. They are dead by the height of the next dry season.

Breeding in the aquarium To breed the egg-hangers put the adults in a tank set up as described on page 14 but with a mop made of a cork and strands of nylon wool (see page 16) instead of top plants. The fishes will lay their eggs on this wool. After a week pick off the eggs—fingers can be used as the eggs are tough—and put them in another container such as a jam jar half-filled with water. The eggs hatch in two to three weeks and can be

fed immediately with newly hatched Brine Shrimp or Micro-worms.

The egg-buryers need a layer of peat 1 in (2·5 cm) thick on the bottom of the tank in which they lay their eggs. About every ten days the peat containing the eggs can be removed with a net and replaced with a fresh layer. Put the peat containing the eggs in a shallow plastic dish and let the water evaporate for about a week until the peat is just dry. Although it is usual to call this 'dried out' peat, it must in fact be slightly moist. This peat should now be put in a screw cap jar clearly labelled with the name of the species and the date 'dried out' and put to incubate in the dark at a temperature of 68–72°F (20–22°C). When the incubation period has elapsed (twelve or sixteen weeks depending upon the species), add 3–4 in (7·5–10 cm) of water and the fry will hatch in a few hours. Feed them on newly hatched Brine Shrimp or Micro-worms.

West African killifishes The genus *Aphyosemion* contains over twenty-five species known to aquarists. All the males are beautifully coloured and have lyre-shaped tail fins, while the females are much duller and have a rounded tail fin. They rarely take dried food.

LYRETAIL, CHOCOLATE LYRETAIL or 'AUSTRALE' *Aphyosemion australe*
Male grows to 2½ in (6·5 cm), female to 2 in (5 cm)
The male is reddish-brown with red spots and an orange edge to the unpaired fins. There is also a gold-coloured variety which has been wrongly named as a separate species, *A. hjerreseni*.

This species is an egg-hanger; use a male with two females for breeding. The optimum temperature for incubating the eggs is 74°F (23°C).

GARDNERI *Aphyosemion gardneri*
Grows to 3 in (7·5 cm)

Black Neons *(Hyphessobrycon
herbertaxelrodi)*

Red-bellied Piranha *(Rooseveltia natteri)*

This is a tough species and one recommended for anyone starting to keep killifishes. There are two different colour varieties, the yellow and the blue. These colour differences are mainly seen in the bands along the edges of the anal, dorsal and caudal fins in the male.

It is an egg-hanger and an easy fish to breed. Although more eggs are obtained by running one male with three females they do very well kept as a separate pair or even as five pairs together.

BLUE GULARIS *Aphyosemion sjoestedti*
Grows to 5 in (12 cm)
This is a large robust fish, the male very easily recognized by his multicoloured trilobate tail fin.

This species of killifish lays its eggs on the bottom among peat fibre. The eggs can then be picked off and incubated in the manner described for egg-hangers, but the incubation period is five to seven weeks. Some aquarists keep these eggs for five to seven weeks in peat which is just moist, as one would the eggs of an egg-buryer. There is evidence to suggest that better and stronger offspring result if the eggs are dried out in this way.

FIRE-MOUTH or RED-CHINNED PANCHAX
Epiplatys dagetti
Male grows to 4 in (10 cm), female to 3½ in (9 cm); West
    Africa
This fish was formerly called *Panchax chaperi* or *Epiplatys chaperi*. It is grey in colour with four or five transverse black bands. The chin and belly in the male are an orange-red.

It is an egg-hanger and can be kept in the community tank where it will patrol the top inch of the water. It will eat dried food.

A good way of breeding this fish is to keep a number of pairs together in a 24 × 12 × 12 (60 × 30 × 30 cm) tank. Remove the eggs from the mops and put them in a jam jar half-full of water in the usual way. The eggs hatch in fourteen to twenty days.

East African killifishes
NOTHOBRANCHIUS GUENTHERI
Male 1¾ in (4·5 cm), female 1½ in (4 cm)
There are over a dozen species of *Nothobranchius* known to aquarists but *N. guentheri* is the most popular. They live in ponds and streams which evaporate during the dry season and are often very muddy, with a lot of surrounding reeds and rushes. In the wild they live less than one year but they do live longer under aquarium conditions. The male is green in colour with many yellow and red spots. It has a bright red caudal fin with a darker border.

This fish is a typical egg-buryer, both parents disappearing into the peat to lay the eggs, which must be dried out for a period of twelve weeks.

PACHYPANCHAX PLAYFAIRI
Grows to 4 in (10 cm); East Africa, Madagascar and the
    Seychelles
The colour is yellow or green with many red spots. This is a large strong fish which will eat dried food and can be kept in the community tank. It is a typical egg-hanger, the eggs hatching in fourteen days.

South American killifishes
DWARF ARGENTINE PEARL FISH *Cynolebias nigripinnis*
Male grows to 1½ in (4 cm), female to 1 in (2·5 cm);
    Argentine
This egg-buryer lives in pools which dry up in the dry season. It is a beautiful fish, the male being dark royal blue with white pearl spots, the female a dull brown. The males are aggressive to the females and even more so to each other.

Keep one male with three females in a typical egg-buryer set up. The eggs have to be dried out for sixteen weeks at 68–70°F (20–21°C). The fry grow extremely rapidly and are sexually mature by eight weeks and dead in eight months.

All the remaining members of this genus and members of the other South American genera *Pterolebias*, *Austrofundulus* and *Rachovia* are egg-buryers.

CHARACINS AND CLOSELY RELATED FAMILIES
Classification In recent years the Family Characidae has been separated from families of somewhat similar fishes which were at one time within the characin family.

Characins *(Pristilla riddlei)*

Since most of these fishes, now in the Families Anostomidae Hemiodontidae, Citharinidae and Gasteropelecidae, need the same sort of treatment from the aquarist as the characins, they have been included in the same section. Characins vary widely in shape and size and over 1,300 species are known. Most species have an additional small unpaired fin—the adipose fin—set between the dorsal and the caudal fins. Some non-characins also have this characteristic.

Distribution and habitat Characins and their relatives are distributed throughout the whole of tropical Africa and Central and South America. The home of the highly popular 'tetras' of the aquarium is the Amazon Basin, where they are found in lakes, ponds, rivers and streams. The area is one of heavy rainfall and, since all mineral salts were dissolved out of the rocks and soil aeons ago, the water is very similar to distilled water in composition. Its colour varies from area to area but much of the water is clear but dark in colour due to rotting vegetation. There is quite a lot of vegetation on the banks of ponds and rivers, but surprisingly little in mid-stream. The water temperature, at 82–86°F (27–30°C), varies little from one part of the year to another. Owing to the large number of characins and the wide area of their distribution, these fishes have filled many different ecological niches, thus producing wide differences within the family; for example, regarding feeding habits, the Red-bellied Piranha (*Rooseveltiella nattereri*) is highly carnivorous and at the other extreme *Myleus* species are herbivorous. There are equally wide differences in the size and shape of different characins. With a few exceptions, of which the piranhas and *Myleus*

species are two, most characins make good community tank fishes. They are hardy and for routine keeping will put up with any reasonable water conditions and take dried foods. They shoal well and display attractively. However, some of the small tetras can be tempted into fin nipping by the long flowing fins of Siamese Fighting Fishes or male Guppies, so do not put prize Fighting Fishes into tanks with these species.

Breeding in the aquarium There are a number of problems in breeding characins but the following method has been found successful with most of the smaller characins. Use a tank of appropriate size—18 × 12 × 12 in (45 × 30 × 30 cm) is large enough for all the small tetras, set up as in fig. 00—and soft water. I find my local tap water of 25 ppm is good enough for all tetras except the Cardinal and the Neon species, and for these two I use water from mountain streams which contains less than 10 ppm of calcium carbonate. Base heating with the thermostat set at 82°F (27°C) should be used. Then put peat, prepared in the usual way, into the tank to a depth of $\frac{1}{8}$ in (3 mm) on the bottom with a large clump of peat fibre. This peat fibre should then be teased out very well so that it takes up half the volume of the tank, enabling the fishes to swim amongst it.

Keep male and female characins for breeding in separate tanks as soon as it is possible to sex them. Feed the adults well and put them into the breeding tank late in the evening, covering it with black polythene to exclude light. Examine the fishes every day to see if they

The Silver Dollar Fish *(Mylossoma argenteum)* is similar to *Metynnis* spp. It is largely herbivorous

Right Bleeding Heart Tetras *(Hyphessobrycon rubrostigma)*. The large fish in the centre of the foreground is a male, the fish to the right is a female.

Below Red Phantom Tetra *(Megalamphodus sweglesi)* male

Blind Cave Fish *(Anoptichthys jordani)*

Black Widows *(Gymnocorymbus ternetzi)*

have spawned; it is usually possible to see the eggs adhering to the peat fibre or scattered into the corners of the tank. The pearly white infertile eggs are most clearly seen. Now remove the parents, but keep the tank covered and dark. If the fishes do not spawn within four days remove them from the breeding tank and put them back in the conditioning tank.

The fry hatch in twenty-four hours and in many species hang vertically from the surface tension film. When disturbed by light they dart and glide to the bottom of the tank. In a few days they become horizontal in position and must now be fed. Better results are obtained by using one of the commercial first foods for egg-layers rather than home-made egg yolk emulsion or infusoria cultures. After about ten days on this diet, newly hatched Brine Shrimp and Micro-worms should be fed. Many species are relatively slow growing.

One problem with characins is that the fishes are relatively difficult to sex. Always buy eight young characins and grow them on together. By observing them daily as they grow it is amazing how nine times out of ten it is possible to separate out the sexes—the females are more rounded, while the dorsal and anal fins are more curved and elongated in the male.

RED-BELLIED PIRANHA *Rooseveltiella nattereri*
Grows to 12 in (30 cm); northern South America
This is one of the species of infamous piranhas. It has conical teeth and especially well developed jaw muscles with which to take big bites out of the flesh of its victims,

which are usually other fishes. In some tributaries of the Amazon the piranhas swim in large shoals and are reported to have reduced a cow, which got into difficulties crossing a river, to a skeleton in a few minutes. It would appear that blood in the water can stimulate such a shoal to a frenzy.

There are also other species of piranha, the *Serresalmus* species and the *Pygocentrus* species. In certain of the warmer states in the USA and in Australia the importation of these fishes is banned so as to prevent their being turned loose and becoming naturalized in local rivers.

Originally aquarists bought one specimen only and kept it on its own, but as experience grows, it now seems possible to keep a number of piranhas of the same size together, providing they are well fed. They appear to like thinly planted tanks with subdued lighting. Their favourite food is live fishes—but they will also eat dead ones—and raw meat, and some aquarists own piranhas which are very fond of tinned cooked meat for dogs.

MARBLED HEADSTANDER *Abramites microcephalus*
Grows to 5 in (13 cm); northern South America
This species is brown in colour with diffuse, irregular, transverse yellow bars. It likes a well-planted aquarium but should be given the larger, tougher plants, such as Cryptocorynes, as it likes to eat algae and fine-leafed plants. It feeds off the bottom and is often found swim-

ming head down or feeding off the bottom in a head-down position, from which it gets its common name.

CARDINAL TETRA *Cheirodon axelrodi*
Grows to 2 in (5 cm); River Negro and its tributaries
This is a favourite aquarium fish, a few of which should be in every aquarist's community tank. A bright blue-green luminous line runs from the mouth to the adipose fin; the body below this line is bright red. The water of its natural habitat is low in mineral content but contains much organic matter—largely decaying fern fronds.

Special efforts have to be made to spawn this fish. Younger fishes spawn more easily than older ones. They are best sexed by looking at them from above, when the female is seen to be more rotund. To breed this fish it is necessary to have very soft water (under 10 ppm) of *p*H 6. After adding the peat fibre I use for spawning characins, I sterilize the whole tank by putting an aquarium heater into it with the thermostat set at 145°F (63°C). Once the water reaches this temperature, it is allowed to cool. So far I have not cracked any tanks using this method of water sterilization! A few days later a pair of well-conditioned fishes is put in and the tank covered with black polythene. If they do not spawn within a week they should be removed and reconditioned. The adults are not fed in the breeding tank. Only a small number of eggs are laid, scattered among the peat fibre and on the bare tank bottom. The eggs hatch in twenty-four hours and are fed in the usual way. The spawnings are small, rarely over twenty-five.

BLACK WIDOW, BLACK TETRA *Gymnocorymbus ternetzi*
Grows to 3 in (7·5 cm); Paraguay, southern Brazil, Argentina and Bolivia
This fish is grey in colour with two black transverse stripes near the head. The male is smaller, with a less deep body and white spots on the caudal fin. A long-finned variety has appeared in recent years. This species rarely grows to 3 in (7·5 cm) under aquarium conditions, but it is hardy, doing best at a temperature of 70–72°F (21–22°C). It is easily bred in the usual characin way.

Genus *HEMIGRAMMUS* This genus contains a number of very attractive and popular aquarium species.

GLOWLIGHT TETRA *Hemigrammus gracilis*
Grows to 1¾ in (4·5 cm); Guyana
This is a silvery fish with a luminous red line running along the lateral line region. The males are thin, at times looking hollow-bellied, with a larger white flashing along the leading edge of the dorsal and anal fins than the females. Mature females are round and plump.

They spawn in the usual characin set up. Males and females which have been well conditioned in separate tanks for a few weeks usually spawn in twenty-four hours. They must be kept in the dark for breeding. Remove the parents when spawning is complete. The fry hatch in twenty-four hours and need egg yolk emulsion for about a week. Keep the tank in the dark until the fry are about ten days old.

BEACON, HEAD and TAIL LIGHT *Hemigrammus ocellifer*
Grows to 1¾ in (4·5 cm); Amazon Basin and the Guianas
This species is greenish-yellow in colour; it derives its common name from the golden spots at the top of the eye and the base of the tail. This is an attractive and peaceful fish which does well in the aquarium and is relatively easy to breed. The females are deeper and plumper than the males, which have a faint horizontal line running across the front edge of the anal fin.

BUENOS AIRES TETRA *Hemigrammus caudovittatus*
Grows to 4 in (10 cm); Argentina
This fish has a silver body with red caudal and anal fins and a diamond-shaped black mark on the caudal peduncle. It tends to be aggressive nipping the fins of other fishes. It can be bred like other characins.

PRETTY TETRA, GARNET TETRA *Hemigrammus pulcher*
Grows to 1¾ in (4·5 cm); Peruvian Amazon
This species is very similar to *H. ocellifer* but has a black bar on the last quarter of the body. The female is a little larger than the male and heavier and more rounded. It is a more difficult species to spawn.

Genus *HYPHESSOBRYCON* This is another genus of brightly coloured popular aquarium tetras. The name 'tetra' comes from the name of the subfamily to which they belong, the Tetragonopterinae or square fins.

BLOOD CHARACINS *Hyphessobrycon callistus* group
There are six subspecies of fishes belonging to this group which were once considered to be separate species. In addition there has probably been a great deal of crossing of these subspecies by aquarists. Irrespective of name all these blood-red tetras are very attractive, especially if kept in well-planted tanks with black backgrounds. All breed in the usual characin way.

BENTOSI TETRA *Hyphessobrycon callistus bentosi*
Grows to 1¼ in (3 cm); Lower Amazon
This subspecies has a faintly marked shoulder spot and faint longitudinal band.

CALLISTUS TETRA *Hyphessobrycon callistus callistus*
Grows to 1½ in (4 cm); River Paraguay
In this subspecies the dorsal fin is almost entirely black, and there is a distinct shoulder marking and well-defined black edge to the anal fin.

ROSY TETRA *Hyphessobrycon callistus rosaceus*
Grows to 2 in (5 cm); Guyana
This fish has no shoulder patch and three quarters of the dorsal fin is black.

COPELANDS TETRA *Hyphessobrycon callistus copelandi*
Grows to 2 in (5 cm); Upper Basin of the Amazon
In this subspecies there is a distinct and elongated shoulder blotch, while the dorsal fin has a broad black centre and white tip.

Marbled Hatchet Fish *(Carnegiella strigata)*

Left Nigger Barbs *(Barbus nigrofasciatus)*

Below Tiger Barb *(Barbus tetrazona)*

HYPHESSOBRYCON CALLISTUS MINOR
Grows to 1½ in (4 cm); Middle Amazon
This fish has a less deep body than *H. c. bentosi* which it otherwise resembles in having a small indistinct shoulder spot and dark longitudinal line.

SERPAE TETRA *Hyphessobrycon callistus serpae*
Grows to 1¾ in (4·5 cm); Middle Amazon
In this subspecies the shoulder spot is indistinct, the dorsal fin is black in the middle with a white tip and the anal fin has a thin black margin.

FLAME or RED TETRA *Hyphessobrycon flammeus*
Grows to 1¼ in (4·5 cm); Brazil
This tetra is very easily kept and probably the easiest to breed. In good condition this is an intensely red fish with two black transverse bars just behind the gills. It is also easy to sex this species as the females become very plump and the males are more highly coloured. Over the years the Flames seen in the UK have been getting less red in colour and it is only rarely that one now sees a Flame with red caudal fins. As this fish is so easy to breed, aquarists should only breed from stock of good colour and cull out all the poorly coloured offspring.

GRIEMI *Hyphessobrycon griemi*
Grows to 1¼ in (3 cm); Brazil
This fish is very close in coloration to the previous species, and is seen to best advantage in well-planted tanks. It breeds in the same way as the rest of the characins but whereas well-conditioned Flames will breed within a few hours of being put in the breeding tank, *Hyphessobrycon griemi* take three to four days before they are ready for spawning.

BLACK NEON *Hyphessobrycon herbertaxelrodi*
Grows to 1½ in (4 cm); Brazil
This species does not really deserve to be called a neon but it is a very attractive fish in a well-planted aquarium. It is greyish-brown in colour with a longitudinal stripe running from the eye to the tail. The lower part of this stripe is black, the upper part a luminous yellow-green. It breeds readily in the usual characin set up although spawnings are not large.

NEON TETRA *Hyphessobrycon innesi*
Grows to 1¾ in (4·5 cm); Peruvian Amazon
This fish was for many years the great favourite for the community tank but has now been pushed into second place by the Cardinal Tetra (*Cheirodon axelrodi*). It is green in colour with a bright blue-green luminous line running from the eye to the adipose fin, the last third of the body being bright red under this line.

The Neon Tetra is difficult to breed and sexing is difficult until the aquarist gains experience, after which it is seen that the female is more plump and the vertical outline of the male is much flatter than in the female. Use young fishes of about 1 in (2·5 cm) in length and soft water (under 10 ppm). In water harder than this the fishes will spawn but the eggs do not hatch. The usual characin set up is used with the tank blacked out. The

Above Arnold's Red-eyed Characin (*Arnoldichthys spilopterus*) is an African species

Opposite *Metynnis schreitmulleri*

fishes may not spawn for three to four days and should be removed after a week if spawning has not occurred. The eggs are scattered all over the peat fibre, and the parents should be removed when spawning is complete.

The fry hatch in twenty-four hours at 82–86°F (27–30°C) and are free swimming by the sixth day. Feed with one of the commercial first foods for egg-layers. At about ten days they should be given newly hatched Brine Shrimp.

LEMON TETRA *Hyphessobrycon pulchripinnis*
Grows to 2 in (5 cm); Brazil
Good Lemon Tetras are very nice fishes but some of those offered for sale are very poor specimens and never develop a good yellow coloration in the leading edges of the dorsal and anal fins, no matter how good the environmental conditions given them. Always try and buy good fishes.

They spawn in the usual characin breeding set up, the eggs not being very adhesive as most of them fall on to the bottom peat. The fry hatch in twenty-four hours at 82°F (27°C) and hang on to the glass, fibre and surface tension film for thirty-six hours. Such foods as egg yolk emulsion should then be given. The tank should be kept covered for about a week. Spawnings are fairly large, with about 100 eggs from one female.

BLEEDING HEART TETRA *Hyphessobrycon rubrostigma*
Grows to 3 in (7·5 cm); Colombia
This fish only grows to 2½ in (6 cm) under aquarium conditions and at this size has a body depth of 1¼ in (3 cm). It has a bright red spot over the heart area from which its common name is derived. It is not easily reared to maturity.

BLACK PHANTOM TETRA *Megalamphodus megalopterus*
Grows to 1½ in (4 cm); Brazil
The two members of this genus are closely related to

Right Cherry Barb *(Barbus titteya)*

Below Zebra Fish *(Brachydanio rerio)*

Harlequin Rasbora *(Rasbora heteromorpha)*

members of the genus *Hyphessobrycon* and need similar water conditions. They will eat dry foods. The male Black Phantom Tetra has a larger dorsal fin and black adipose and anal fins; these are red in the female. The body colour in both sexes is a dusty black. It spawns in the same way as *Hemigrammus* and *Hyphessobrycon* species.

RED PHANTOM TETRA *Megalamphodus sweglesi*
Grows to 1¼ in (3 cm); Colombia
This species is similar in many ways to the Serpae Tetra, but it is not as large and has a characteristic black blotch on its sides. It is also more transparent. The male has a larger dorsal fin but the earliest sign of sexual differentiation is a white spot right at the tip of the dorsal fin in the female. These fishes swim in shoals near the bottom and then make quick darts at food as it sinks from the top—a few fishes at first and then the whole shoal.

It is much easier to breed this species by putting several fishes in the breeding tank together—say two males and four females—than by using one pair only.

SWORDTAIL CHARACIN *Corynopoma riisei*
Grows to 2½ in (6 cm); northern Venezuela and Trinidad
This is an interesting characin but it is inclined to fin nipping. The male has a long spoon-shaped appendage on the gill cover which is white, with the spoon-shaped end black during breeding. This appendage is used by the male to 'stroke' the female during courtship.

Fertilization is thought to be internal, the male transferring a capsule of sperm to the female's oviduct where it is retained until the laying of the eggs. The female once mated may now spawn many times without the further presence of the male. After fertilization the female swims away from the male and lays eggs on broad-leafed plants. She then maintains a guard over them, frequently moving them to fresh positions. The fry hatch in thirty-six hours and are guarded for a few more days by the female.

SPLASHING CHARACIN *Copeina arnoldi*
Grows to 3 in (7·5 cm); Amazon
This species is reddish-brown in colour, the male having larger and redder fins. It is not only a very different characin in shape from the tetras but has an unusual method of breeding.

Set up a characin breeding tank but without the peat fibre and only 4 in (10 cm) of water depth. Place a piece of slate or roughened plastic in such a way that it is half out of the water, leaning against the side of the tank. The fishes leap out of the water and lay an adherent egg on the slate above the surface. This process is repeated until a mass of eggs is laid on the underside of the slate. The male now takes up a position under the eggs and splashes water on them until they hatch three days later.

METYNNIS ROOSEVELTI
Grows to 6 in (15 cm) and 4 in (10 cm) deep; Amazon
This silvery fish is one of the disc-shaped characins and,

Penguin Fish *(Thayeria obliqua)* with *Daphnia*

as it is a shoaling species, needs a large tank. It is herbivorous and eats aquarium plants so should be given lettuce and spinach in its diet. It has been spawned in the aquarium.

BLIND CAVE FISH *Anoptichthys jordani*
Grows to 3½ in (9 cm); underground pools and streams near San Luis Potosi in Mexico

This is a true cave fish in which, owing to generations of living in complete darkness, the eyes have atrophied. Though blind the fish gets about well and catches live foods using its increased senses of touch and smell. It is pale pink in colour and can be kept in the normal lighted aquarium. Occasionally one sees this species very well displayed in 'cave-like' settings in public aquaria.

It can be bred in the usual characin way, the parents being removed as soon as spawning is completed. Eggs hatch in about three days and the fry are free swimming in another three.

EMPEROR TETRA *Nematobrycon palmeri*
Grows to 3 in (7·5 cm); Colombia

A black line runs from the eye to the tail fin in this fish. Above the line the body is grey-blue, but below the line the body is yellow. The male is easily recognized by his three-lobed caudal fin.

It is best bred by keeping three pairs in an 18 × 10 × 10 in (45 × 25 × 25 cm) tank set up in the usual way. After a week move the fishes on to another tank. They lay a few eggs each day and do not seem to bother the newly hatched fry.

PENGUIN FISH *Thayeria obliqua*
Grows to 2½ in (6 cm); Amazon

This peaceful fish swims with its tail down. It is silver-coloured with a black line running from the region of the lateral line over its last third down into the lower lobe of the caudal fin. The female can be distinguished because she is deeper and more rounded than the male. It breeds in the usual characin way.

CONGO TETRA *Micralestes interruptus*
Grows to 4½ in (11·5 cm); Congo Basin

This fish is basically grey in colour but the large scales reflect beautiful yellow and green colours in adult fishes. The male is easily recognized as it is larger and brighter coloured, with a greatly extended dorsal fin and the middle rays of the caudal fin extended. This species needs large tanks with soft peaty water and as it eats insect foods in nature, these should be given if available.

It spawns in the usual characin manner, the eggs falling through the fibre on to the peat compost as they are non-adhesive. Eggs take five days to hatch.

MARBLED HATCHET FISH *Carnegiella strigata*
Grows to 1¾ in (4·5 cm); Amazon and Orinoco regions

This fish has a very characteristic shape, with large pectoral fins. It lives in forest pools and when chased by other fishes shoots out of the water and glides for long distances through the air. It has not yet spawned in captivity and is difficult to sex.

BECKFORD'S PENCIL FISH *Nannostomus beckfordi*
Grows to 2 in (5 cm); Amazon

The genus *Nannostomus* belongs to the Family Hemiodontidae and its members make good community aquarium fishes. This member of the pencil fish group is easily sexed; all the fins in the female are colourless and she is more rounded, while the male has red on the lower lobe of the caudal fin and on the anal fin.

For breeding, leave about a dozen adults in a 36 × 12 × 12 in (90 × 30 × 30 cm) tank with two clumps of peat fibre at each end. When the adults have spawned it is possible to remove the fry, which cling to the glass— usually within 3 in (7·5 cm) of the waterline—by catching them with a pipette after the tank has been darkened for some hours. The parents lay a few eggs daily.

CYPRINIDS
Classification The Family Cyprinidae contains over 1,500 species, some of which are important food fishes. In this family are the important genera *Barbus*, *Danio* and *Rasbora* and a number of species of different genera collectively known to aquarists as minnows. In general the fishes of this family are conventionally fish-shaped,

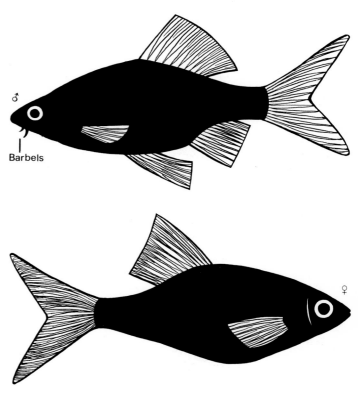

Barbs, carp and minnows *(Barbus comingi)*

have large scales and are very quick moving. A number of species have one or two pairs of barbels which are used to help them search for food among the gravel. The barbels have special sense organs called taste buds and also a network of free nerve endings so that both taste and touch sensations are used in the choice of food. This family contains some very large fishes, for example *Barbus tor*, which grows to 8 ft (2½ m) in length, but most fishes of interest to the aquarist are in the 2–3 in (5–7·5 cm) range.

Clown Rasboras *(Rasbora kalochroma)* with male above

Left Scissortail *(Rasbora trilineata)*

Below White Cloud Mountain Minnows
(Tanichthys albonubes)

Distribution and habitat This family is very widely distributed in nature except for Australasia, South America and the cold regions of Canada, northern Europe and northern Asia. It includes many of the European angler's coarse fish such as Carp (*Cyprinus carpio*), Orfe (*Leuciscus idus*), Dace (*Leuciscus leuciscus*), Roach (*Rutilus rutilus*) and Tench (*Tinca tinca*) and the Goldfish (*Carassius auratus*).

Barbs Though some American authorities have divided the genus *Barbus* into a number of new genera—*Puntius*, *Barbodes* and *Capoeta*—all barbs are classified here under the genus *Barbus*.

Barbs are very widely distributed in the Old World and occupy a large number of habitats in rivers, lakes and pools. They are not demanding as far as water conditions go but prefer clear tanks. In nature they often live in shoals and therefore look better if a number of individuals are kept together in the tank. They take dried foods easily but a few species are likely to nibble plants.

To breed barbs condition the male and female separately for about two to three weeks and the female will be seen to get plump. Set up a $24 \times 12 \times 12$ in ($60 \times 30 \times 30$ cm) tank to a depth of 6–8 in (15–20 cm) using fairly soft water (no harder than 100 ppm). Into this place a breeding trap made of $\frac{1}{4}$ in (6 mm) plastic mesh which is almost as large as the tank, but about 1 in (2·5 cm) less in depth than the tank. A layer of peat fibre, teased out very fine, should be placed on the bottom of the breeding trap. The parents are put in late at night and usually spawn within three days. If not, they should be removed and reconditioned.

When spawning takes place the pair chase up and down the tank, then lie side by side among the peat fibre when the eggs and milt are emitted. Though the eggs are adhesive the vigorous swimming of the male causes most of the eggs to fall through the trap. Without a breeding trap the parents will eat the eggs when spawning has been completed, but even with a trap they should be removed at this point. Two layers of marbles or $\frac{1}{3}$ in (8 mm) diameter pebbles can be used to protect the eggs.

The eggs hatch in about thirty-six hours when the fry will be seen clinging to the sides of the glass. They become free swimming in about another two days and can then be fed egg yolk emulsion. At the end of a week they should be given newly hatched Brine Shrimp and Microworms. Spawnings can be large, so poor or abnormal fry should be culled.

ARULIUS BARB *Barbus arulius*
Grows to 5 in (12 cm); south-eastern India
This is a very typical barb with large scales and one pair of barbels on the upper jaw. It looks very good with light falling on it from the front. In these conditions the brownish body takes on a reddish lustre and the light reflects the greenish spots on the scales. In a mature male there are elongations to the rays of the dorsal fin.

It spawns in the usual barb set up. The eggs are large—$\frac{1}{8}$ in (3 mm) in diameter—and after hatching the fry remain on the bottom for two days followed by a further

Knife Fish *(Xenomystus nigri)* – a cyprinid

Left Red-tailed Black Shark *(Labeo bicolor)*

Below Sucking Catfish *(Plecostomus plecostomus)*

two days on the sides of the glass. By this time the fry are large and can be given newly hatched Brine Shrimp.

ROSY BARB *Barbus conchonius*
Grows to 5½ in (14 cm); northern India
This very popular fish is the easiest of all the barbs to breed. It is olive-green in colour with a black spot towards the tail fin, the male only having an area of black on the dorsal and anal fins. In breeding condition the male develops a rosy colour all over the body.

CLOWN BARB *Barbus everetti*
Grows to 5½ in (14 cm); Singapore and Borneo
This fish is a dull yellow in colour with four black but indistinct markings on the body. The female grows longer than the male and is plumper and less bright in colour. It breeds in the usual barb manner. This species likes vegetable food in its diet and will eat plants, particularly pieces of *Myriophyllum*.

FILAMENT BARB *Barbus filamentosus*
Grows to 6 in (15 cm); south-west India
This is a fish which changes its appearance as it grows up. The young fishes are very brightly coloured, yellow and black, but as they mature become more olive-coloured with the bars fading to one black blotch above the anal fin. The adult male has elongations of the rays of the dorsal fins.

They need a tank 24 × 12 × 12 in (60 × 30 × 30 cm) or 36 × 12 × 12 in (90 × 30 × 30 cm) for breeding and as breeding traps of this size are not always available use a bare tank with a lot of teased out clumps of peat fibres. Remove the parents as soon as spawning has finished. Feed the fry on newly hatched Brine Shrimp when they become free swimming.

GOLDEN DWARF BARB *Barbus gelius*
Grows to 1½ in (4 cm); central India and Bengal
This is one of the smallest barbs and has no barbels. It is not a particularly brightly coloured fish but it makes no special demands and is not such an extrovert as many of the larger barbs. It has a gold-coloured body and an irregular number of black patches on its sides; the female is larger than the male and well rounded when mature.

They breed in the usual barb manner. The eggs hatch in twenty-four hours and the fry hang on to the peat fibre and the glass for another forty-eight. They should be fed on one of the commercial first foods for egg-layers.

SPANNER or 'T' BARB *Barbus lateristriga*
Grows to 6½ in (16·5 cm); Malaysia
This is a widely distributed barb with a number of colour varieties depending upon where it comes from. The commonest is a pale yellow with two transverse black bars and a short longitudinal black bar which comes from the tail to meet them, thus forming a 'T'. Sexing is not easy with this fish and the deeper body of the female is the most reliable feature to use as a guide. It is best spawned in a 36 × 12 × 12 in (90 × 30 × 30 cm) tank because of its larger size.

EMBER BARB *Barbus melanampyx*
Grows to 3 in (7·5 cm); India
This is a relatively rare import which should become popular as both male and female are a reddish-pink, becoming more red when in breeding condition.

It can be bred in the usual barb way, but put two females with one male as, like the Cherry Barb (*B. titteya*), the male is a hard driver.

NIGGER, BLACK RUBY or PURPLE-HEADED BARB *Barbus nigrofasciatus*
Grows to 2 in (5 cm); southern Ceylon
In non-peak condition this is not a very attractive fish compared with the Tiger Barb (*B. tetrazona*), for example, but in breeding condition the males are magnificent, the whole front half of the body a bright red. It is easy to sex this species when adult as the females are not as colourful. They should be bred in the same way as other barbs.

CHECKER BARB *Barbus oligolepis*
Grows to 2 in (5 cm); Sumatra
This is another of the small popular aquarium barbs with no bad features. It is orange-yellow in colour with irregular black blotches on its sides. The males have reddish-orange fins edged with black, whereas the fins in the females are yellowish without the black edges. It is more difficult to breed but good conditioning and a careful selection of mature pairs usually result in a spawning.

SCHUBERT'S BARB *Barbus 'schuberti'*
Grows to 3 in (7·5 cm)
This name is not an accepted scientific one and, as this fish is not found in the wild, its source is not known for certain. It is variously reported as a golden variety of *B. semifasciolatus* or a golden variety of *B. sachsi* or even as a hybrid. It is a most attractive fish, both easy to keep and easy to breed. The male is slimmer than the female and has a row of black spots along the body, whereas the female only has one or two spots.

TINFOIL BARB *Barbus schwanenfeldi*
Grows to 14 in (35·5 cm); Malaysia, Thailand and Sumatra
A silvery-yellow body with bright orange fins, some of which are edged with black, make this a handsome fish. It is a barb for the specialist or for the collector of big fishes and really good specimens can be seen in public aquaria. They are good leapers and eat plants, so are best kept in tanks with a gravel compost and rocks for decoration, and given their vegetables in the form of lettuce, spinach or squashed cooked peas.

Spawning takes place in the usual way in a 36 × 12 × 12 in (90 × 30 × 30 cm) aquarium with bunches of peat fibre as spawning medium.

TICTO BARB *Barbus ticto*
Grows to 4 in (10 cm); India and Ceylon
This is a close relative of *B. stoliczkanus* (Stoliczka's Barb) but grows larger and has an incomplete lateral line; they

Nigger Barbs *(Barbus nigrofasciatus)*

are, nevertheless, very similar in appearance—both with a general body colour of pale yellow, the males only having a bright red dorsal fin edged with black and with a black crescent in the centre. This species breeds in the usual barb way.

TIGER BARB *Barbus tetrazona*
Grows to 3 in (7·5 cm); Sumatra and Borneo
This is the most popular of aquarium barbs and maintains its bright appearance at all times. It has a golden-yellow body with four black stripes—at the eye, in front of the dorsal, just behind the dorsal and at the caudal peduncle. The male has a red nose and is slimmer and brighter coloured than the female. An albino variety has appeared in recent years.

Condition and spawn the fishes in the usual way using a breeding trap. After forty-eight hours the fry need egg yolk emulsion for a few days and then newly hatched Brine Shrimp. Mutants with two tails or 'pop' eyes are sometimes to be found among large spawnings.

CHERRY BARB *Barbus titteya*
Grows to 2 in (5 cm); Ceylon
This is a beautiful and peaceful small barb which is very suitable for the community tank or for the beginner. During spawning the cherry-maroon colour in the male becomes very intense. Breed in the usual way but as the male is very ardent, put two females to each male.
There are a few African barbs which are known to the aquarist but there are numbers of others not yet im-

ported which will in the future make attractive specimens.

TWO-SPOT AFRICAN BARB *Barbus puckelli*
Grows to 2¾ in (7 cm); River Congo
This fish has been known in Britain as *B. bimaculatus*. It is dull gold in colour with a small black spot on the caudal peduncle and at the base of the dorsal fin, the female being large and more rounded than the male. An albino variety of this species also occurs. This species is very easy to breed.

Danios There are two genera in this very popular group of fishes—*Brachydanio* and *Danio*—which are found throughout tropical India, Burma, the Malay Peninsula and Sumatra. They live in rivers, streams, rice paddies, pools and lakes and are often found in large shoals. Most species possess two pairs of barbels. They are all extremely active, using the whole depth of the tank and dashing from one end to the other. They are good community tank fishes, not eating plants, and taking both live and dried foods.

All of them can be bred in the same way, using a breeding trap with some well teased out peat fibre along the bottom. The eggs are non-adhesive and fall through the trap on to the bottom. Some people prefer to use two layers of marbles along the bottom of the tank rather than a breeding trap (see page 16).

PEARL DANIO *Brachydanio albolineatus*
Grows to 2 in (5 cm); India, Burma and Malaya
This is a peaceful and very typical danio which is very easy to breed. It is pearl-coloured with an orange line

Right Tiger Scat (*Scatophagus argus*) in
aggressive display

Below Mudskipper (*Periophthalmus*)

surmounting a blue line running from the middle of the body back to the tail fin. The female is larger and more rotund than the male and is less highly coloured. A golden colour variety also occurs.

LEOPARD DANIO Brachydanio frankei
Grows to 2½ in (6·5 cm); India
This has become a very popular fish since it was first imported in 1963. It is blue-grey in colour, covered in darker irregular spots. The female is larger and plumper when mature, with a silvery-coloured belly. It breeds in the usual danio way.

SPOTTED DANIO Brachydanio nigrofasciatus
Grows to 2 in (5 cm); Burma
This is another attractive fish which in a small shoal enhances the appearance of a community tank. It is brown in colour above a double blue line running from the gill cover to the tail fin and below the lines has dark spots on a yellowish background. It is not so easy to breed as some of the other species.

ZEBRA FISH Brachydanio rerio
Grows to 2 in (5 cm); India
This is a fish which is kept at some time by all aquarists. It is covered in blue stripes which run from the nose to the end of the tail against a silvery background. It looks attractive and is the nearest thing in the fish world to perpetual motion. A golden-coloured variety in which the background is gold rather than silver now exists. It has no special requirements and breeds very easily.

BENGAL DANIO Danio devario
Grows to 4 in (10 cm); north-west India
This is a hardy, larger fish but it has the same peaceful habits as Brachydanio species and is equally active. It has a silver-blue body, the blue being concentrated over the flanks with a number of thin iridescent longitudinal and vertical yellow stripes. The female is plumper and has greater body depth than the male but is less brightly coloured. It can be bred in the usual danio manner.

GIANT DANIO Danio malabaricus
Grows to 5 in (13 cm); Ceylon and India
Although this robust fish is larger than Brachydanio species, it is peaceful and can be kept in the community tank. It is silver on the back and belly with three blue longitudinal stripes alternating with four thinner pale orange ones. The female is deeper-bodied and the central blue stripe turns upwards in the region of the caudal fin. It is bred in the usual way but the eggs are adhesive.

Rasboras The genus Rasbora contains species differing considerably in appearance which are widely distributed, from East Africa through South-east Asia as far as China, to the East Indies and the Philippines. Most of the species known to the hobbyist come from the Malay Peninsula. They live in rivers and lakes in large shoals and a number of species spawn in shoals.

Although there are some species which are exceptionally hard to breed, normally they are not difficult if given the right conditions. They require soft, acid water (pH 6·5) of a depth of about 6 in (15 cm); the temperature should be 75–80°F (24–27°C). Do not use a breeding trap but place clumps of peat fibre in the middle of the tank and at each corner. The semi-adhesive eggs are laid among the peat fibre.

The fry hatch in three days, and should be given egg yolk emulsion for a few days and then newly hatched Brine Shrimp. Adults eat both dried and live foods.

RED-TAILED RASBORA Rasbora borapetensis
Grows to 2½ in (6·5 cm); Thailand
This fish has a black stripe from the gill cover to the caudal peduncle with a thinner golden line above it. The back is yellow-green and the belly is silver. The male is slightly smaller and slimmer than the female.

To breed these fishes the males and females should be well conditioned separately and the best male and female placed in a 24×12×12 in (60×30×30 cm) tank with water of pH 6·5, hardness 10 ppm, at a temperature of 82°F (27°C) and three clumps of well teased out peat fibre.

GIANT or GREATER SCISSORTAIL Rasbora caudimaculata
Grows to 8 in (20 cm); Malay Peninsula and Sumatra
This fish is not often seen in the UK. It has the same scissor-like movements of its tail when swimming as its smaller relative, R. trilineata. The body is silver in colour with a violet iridescence and a very attractive red coloration on the tail fins. There is a faint longitudinal stripe. The female is deeper bodied and more rounded than the male. This species has not yet been bred in captivity.

ELEGANT or TWO-SPOT RASBORA Rasbora elegans
Grows to 5 in (13 cm); Malay Peninsula and nearby islands
This is another silver-coloured danio. Two spots, one on the body beneath the dorsal fin, which is rectangular in shape, and one on the caudal peduncle, characterize this fish. The male is smaller and slimmer than the female, and brighter coloured. It breeds in the usual way, laying adhesive eggs.

HARLEQUIN RASBORA Rasbora heteromorpha
Grows to 1¾ in (4·5 cm); Malay Peninsula, Sumatra and Java
This is a popular fish which looks best of all in a small shoal. It has a violet-red body, with a large black triangle covering its posterior half. Sexing is difficult, but with observation and experience it is possible to recognize the brighter, slimmer males.

It is difficult to breed. In nature this species is always found in shoals and is thought to be a shoal-spawner.

CLOWN RASBORA Rasbora kalochroma
Grows to 3 in (7·5 cm); Malay Peninsula
This fish was imported into the UK for the first time in 1970. It is pinkish-red in colour with a large black spot

behind the gill cover and a larger black spot above the anal fin. In shape it is more like a copeina than a rasbora, the male having black edges to his pelvic and anal fins. It is said to spawn in typical rasbora fashion.

PIGMY, DWARF or SPOTTED RASBORA *Rasbora maculata*
Grows to 1 in (2·5 cm); Malay Peninsula and Sumatra
This is a very small fish but most attractive given the right conditions, a dark background to the tank and sunlight from the front. In this environment the back is reddish coloured, fading to orange on the belly, and there is a large black spot on the side. The female is more rounded and has two black spots near the vent.

It spawns best in soft (10 ppm) water with a *p*H of 6·3 and peat clumps as the spawning medium. The fry need egg yolk emulsion for the first week.

RED LINE or RED-STRIPED RASBORA *Rasbora pauciperforata*
Grows to 2½ in (6·5 cm); Sumatra and the Malay Peninsula
This is the 'Glowlight' of the *Rasbora* genus, with a red luminous line running from the eye to the caudal fin. For spawning it prefers a tank with a small amount of peat on the bottom and well teased out clumps of peat

fibre. The newly hatched fry need egg yolk emulsion for a few days.

SCISSORTAIL or THREE-LINED RASBORA *Rasbora trilineata*
Grows to 6 in (15 cm); Malaysia
A very distinctly forked tail which it opens and shuts like a pair of scissors accounts for the common name of this fish. It is silver with a thin black line from gill cover to caudal peduncle, the female being plumper and deeper bodied. It spawns in the usual rasbora way, laying semi-adhesive eggs on the peat fibre.

FIRE RASBORA *Rasbora vaterifloria*
Grows to 1½ in (4 cm); Ceylon
In this species the back is orange-purple, with the belly and all the fins orange. The females are less colourful and more rounded than the males.

It spawns in the usual rasbora manner, laying semi-adhesive eggs on the peat fibre; many of them fall to the tank bottom.

Minnows
WHITE CLOUD MOUNTAIN MINNOW *Tanichthys albonubes*
Grows to 1¼ in (3 cm); Canton, China
The dorsal fin is yellow near the body but the rest of the fin is red.

As this fish comes from outside the tropics it breeds

Catfish *(Pimelodella gracilis)*

readily at 70–72°F (21–22°C). Breeding is very easy; if a few mature pairs are left together in a well-planted tank and fed well they will lay eggs intermittently for days. The fry, which stick to the glass for a few days, can be picked up in a medicine dropper and put into another tank. Give them egg yolk emulsion as a first food. In my experience this fish is very susceptible to Velvet disease.

Other Cyprinids There are a number of other Cyprinidae which are very popular in the tropical aquarium. Many of them have been given the popular name 'sharks' because of the shape of the caudal fins. They are in no way related to marine sharks which are primitive fishes belonging to a completely different order.

SILVER or BALA SHARK *Balanteocheilus*
Grows to 14 in (35·5 cm); Thailand, Sumatra and Borneo
Silver with black fins, this is a very attractive fish which does a great deal of scavenging off the bottom. Aquarium specimens have grown to 8 in (20 cm). It is said to be a very good jumper. It has not yet bred in captivity.

RED-TAILED BLACK SHARK *Labeo bicolor*
Grows to 5 in (13 cm); Thailand
This is a very attractive velvet-black fish with a red tail. It defends its territory strongly against its own fellows but is no trouble in the community tank.

RED-FINNED SHARK *Labeo erythrura*
Grows to 4½ in (11·5 cm); Thailand
This species is not as impressively coloured as the other 'sharks' and is a middle-water swimmer. It is greyish-brown with bright red fins, the male having a black edge to the anal fin. It has been spawned in captivity.

BLACK SHARK *Morulius chrysophekadion*
Grows to 20 in (51 cm); Thailand
This is a very long-lived fish which starts off by being black but becomes more brownish as it gets older. It has two pairs of barbels and will eat algae off plants and the aquarium glass. The sex differences are not known.

FLYING FOX *Epalzeorhynchus kallopterus*
Grows to 5 in (13 cm); Sumatra and Borneo
This is another unusual and attractive fish which spends a lot of time near the bottom. It also uses its pectoral fins as a 'prop' to support itself when resting upon the bottom. It eats algae. As this fish quarrels with other members of its species, keep only one to a tank.

THE CATFISHES
There are species of catfish from at least seventeen different families which have been kept at some time by fish keepers. They are very widely distributed and vary very widely in appearance and behaviour. Some of them are kept by aquarists for their bizarre shapes, some are kept for their bizarre habits and many are kept for the good quality they have of acting as scavengers by eating up surplus food fed to the aquarium.

Catfishes *(Corydoras arcuatus)*

Callichthyidae This family is characterized by the bony plates on the flanks, and one to two pairs of barbels on the upper jaw. Its members come from South America and Trinidad where they live in shoals in slowly moving water. Some of them, by using their pectoral fins as legs and the intestine as an accessory respiratory organ, leave the water and 'walk' on mud flats and sandbanks. In the aquarium they turn over the mulm and gravel, eating up unwanted food debris, and form a good scavenging service.

ARMOURED CATFISH *Callichthys callichthys*
Grows to 7 in (18 cm); South America and Trinidad
This species has armoured plates on its sides and also over its head. It is a night-feeding fish. Its breeding biology is interesting; the male is said to blow a bubble nest among the leaves of floating plants, and after spawning to take care of the eggs.

BRONZE CATFISH *Corydorus aeneus*
Grows to 2¾ in (7 cm); South America and Trinidad
This is an attractive fish in a number of ways—it is a good scavenger, withstands a wide temperature range, has a method of air breathing if it wants to and the faculty of rolling its eyes independently. It is greenish-brown in colour with a lighter coloured belly. This fish does breed in the aquarium, the female laying adhesive eggs on plants, rocks and glass walls.

Loricariidae This is another large family of catfishes which possess armour. They have a sucking mouth which enables them to cling on to the stones in the small fast-flowing streams in which they live. In the wild these catfishes feed predominantly upon algae. Vegetable foods are therefore an essential constituent of their diet.

Top Bronze Catfish *(Corydoras aeneus)*

Left *Loricaria parva*

Above *Scatophagus argus*

Right Sucker Loach *(Gyrinocheilus aymonieri)*
Below Elephant Nose Fish *(Gnathonemus petersi)*
Bottom Malayan Angel *(Monodoactylus argenteus)*

MIDGET or DWARF SUCKER CATFISH *Otocinclus affinis*
Grows to 2 in (5 cm); south-east Brazil
This small catfish is a grey-brown colour with a longitudinal wide dark band and a dark spot at the base of the tail. The food of this fish also consists of algae. The lips form a circular sucking organ.

The female lays single eggs, pressing them on to the under-surface of broad-leafed plants where the egg is fertilized by the male. The fry must have plenty of algae-filled water if they are to be reared successfully.

PLEOCOSTOMUS SUCKER CATFISH *Pleocostomus commersoni*
Grows to 16 in (11 cm); South America
This is an undemanding fish which is an algae-eater and will remove algae from Cryptocorynes in a fine manner, but it may damage fine-leafed plants. It can grow very large. It is grey-brown in colour with dark blotches.

Siluridae
KRYPTOPTERUS BICIRRHIS The Glass Catfish
Grows to 4 in (10 cm); India
This is an almost transparent catfish which swims in mid-water. It does best in a small shoal and needs live foods. It has not yet spawned in captivity.

OTHER SPECIES
This section consists of fishes from a large number of widely different families, some of the fish requiring special conditions of water and temperature.

Scatophagidae The members of this family, which come from South-east Asia, Indonesia and northern Australia, are found in both salt and brackish coastal waters. It is thought that they spawn on coral reefs, the young then moving into the fresh water at the mouths of rivers until adult, when they return to the sea.

TIGER SCAT, LEOPARD SCAT *Scatophagus argus*
Grows to 12 in (30 cm); India and South-east Asia
This is a very attractive disc-shaped fish, yellow in colour with brown or black spots. It has not been bred in captivity. It does well in hard (100–200 ppm) water with a pH of 7·2–7·4. Some authorities add salt but I have tried varying mixtures of salt water with fresh water and find fresh water as described above the most satisfactory. A group of scats on their own are very aggressive, the smallest one being killed off in turn until only the largest is left, but, surprisingly, if well fed, they do not seem to bother other fishes. They eat all foods, but rarely grow above 6 in (15 cm) in the aquarium.

Monodactylidae The members of this family resemble the angelfishes in shape and colour. They live in the sea and in brackish waters at the mouths of rivers.

MONODACTYLUS ARGENTEUS (Malayan Angel or Fingerfish, Mono)
Grows to 9 in (23 cm); Malaysia to East Africa
This silver fish has two black transverse stripes and, as it comes from coastal regions, can be kept in salt water or in a mixture of four parts of fresh water to one of salt water. It eats live foods only and has never been bred in captivity.

Gyrinocheilidae
SUCKER LOACH or CHINESE ALGAE EATER
Gyrinocheilus aymonieri
Grows to 10 in (25 cm) in the wild; Thailand
This species lives in fast-flowing streams. It does not have a swim bladder, the lack of which helps it to stay near the bottom where it can hang on to rocks with its sucker-like mouth. It also has a modification of its opercular opening; this is divided into two horizontally, and water is taken in through one half and expelled through the other. This adaptation prevents the fish from having to take in water through its mouth, which it needs to hold on to the rocks. In the aquarium, as in the wild, it is a vegetarian and does a good job keeping plants and front glass free of unsightly algae. Rare chance spawnings have occurred in tanks in which there is a combination of fast filtration and good lighting promoting flourishing algal growth. This replicates to some extent the fishes' natural surroundings.

Mormyridae These most peculiar freshwater fishes come from the Nile valley and the rest of Africa south of the Sahara. Some larger lake specimens are important food fishes. Many of them are nocturnal and have an electric organ which can give out weak discharges. A number of species have a trunk-shaped proboscis on the jaw which serves as a feeler and which gives these species one of their common names, the Elephant Nose or Trunk Fishes.

ELEPHANT NOSE FISH *Gnathonemus petersi*
Grows to 9 in (23 cm); West Africa
This bottom-feeding species has a 'trunk' projecting from the chin. The body, which narrows very sharply behind the dorsal fin, is dark brown with two clear irregular transverse bars between the dorsal and anal fins. This is a peaceful, nocturnal fish.

Cobitidae This family consists of a number of genera; its tropical members come from the Middle East, India, South-east Asia, Indonesia and Indo-China. In Africa, these fishes are found only in Morocco and Ethiopia. The family is divided into two main groups, the loaches and the spiny loaches. The spiny loaches have a simple or perforated spine below and in front of each eye which can be erected and helps to protect the fish against predators. They are all bottom-living fish.

COOLIE or LEOPARD LOACH
Acanthophthalmus kuhlii
Grows to $3\frac{1}{2}$ in (9 cm); South-east Asia
This fish is worm-like in shape but very attractive with its yellow and black bands. It likes a well-planted tank and some hiding places among rocks. It eats all foods and is more active at night. Accidental spawnings have been reported.

Top Archerfish *(Toxotes jaculator)*
Right *Chanda wolfii*
Above Arawana *(Osteoglossum bicirrhosum)*

CLOWN LOACH or TIGER BOTIA *Botia macrocanthus*
Grows to 8 in (20 cm); Sumatra and Borneo
This species is yellow with three broad transverse black bands. Aquarium specimens rarely grow to more than 4 in (10 cm). It is more active during the day than many other fishes in this family and swims up and down the glass of the aquarium very happily. It eats all foods, although I have had one specimen which was addicted to nibbling the growing points of the delicate-leafed species of plants.

Centropomidae
INDIA GLASSFISH *Chanda ranga*
Grows to 2 in (5 cm); northern India and South-east Asia
The genus *Chanda* was formerly called *Ambassis. C. ranga* is the best known of the glassfish family. As its common name implies, it is very transparent but sexing is easy as the male has a light blue trailing edge to its dorsal fin. It eats live foods only.

This species spawns very easily. I use the local tap water (25 ppm) with two teaspoons of salt to ten litres of water, with a teased out clump of peat fibre placed on the bare bottom of the tank. When a pair of well-conditioned adults is put in the tank a fast-darting courtship ensues. After the spawning is over remove the parents.

The fry hatch in twenty-four hours and are some of the smallest of fish fry; they are best fed with green water containing *Euglena* or if this is not available use one of the commercial first foods for egg-layers.

Osteoglossidae This is a most unusual family of fishes with very large bony scales. It contains one of the largest tropical fish, *Arapaima gigas*, which grows to 12 ft (3 m), and many public aquaria have a specimen.

ARAWANA *Osteoglossum bicirrhosum*
Grows to 18 in (45 cm); the Guianas
A large mouth directed upwards, two forked barbels standing out from the end of the chin, snake-like swimming movements and a predatory nature characterize this fish. It is a dull grey-green in colour with large iridescent scales. It is a species for the collector.

Periophthalmidae
MUDSKIPPER *Periophthalmus barbarus*
Grows to 6 in (15 cm); Red Sea, East Africa, southern Asia and Australia
In the wild this species lives in the brackish water in muddy tidal flats and mangrove swamps, in which it walks when the tide goes out. It needs a specially large tank with shallow water and sloping gravel coming out of the water so that it has some land to walk on. Add two teaspoons of salt to ten litres of water. The tank must have a tight lid so as to keep the air moist.

Rock Beauty *(Holocanthus tricolor)* at top
with Four-eyed Butterflyfish *(Chaetodon
capistratus)* and Spanish Hogfish *(Bodianus
rufus)*

MARINE FISHES
GRAHAM COX

EQUIPMENT FOR THE MARINE AQUARIUM

Setting up a marine aquarium poses a rather special set of problems for two main reasons. Firstly, the chemical nature of sea water is very different from that of fresh water. Secondly, the sea is in many ways a far more stable environment than fresh water and the majority of its inhabitants are adapted to make the most of a much narrower range of conditions.

THE CHOICE OF TANK

The most important point to bear in mind is that salt water is extremely corrosive; it will rapidly attack any exposed metal surface, weakening the structure and—more immediately important—allowing the toxic products of metal corrosion to pollute the aquarium. This determines the kinds of materials which may be used in the construction of a tank. The strength of the materials used depends upon the pressure to which the tank is subjected. The pressure within a liquid increases with depth but is independent of the other physical dimensions. Also the pressure acts in all directions—it presses outwards against the sides as well as downwards against the base. A tank which is 10 in (25 cm) deep will not require thicker glass if it is 36 in (90 cm) long by 18 in (45 cm) wide than if it is 18 in (45 cm) long by 10 in (25 cm) wide. But any 18 in (45 cm) deep tank will certainly require thicker glass than any 10 in (25 cm) deep tank.

All-glass construction The all-glass tank, which is essentially five plates of glass bonded together with silicone rubber adhesive, readily meets the requirements of non-corrosibility and non-toxicity. For the aquarist who intends to build his own tank the following points should be borne in mind. The glass surfaces to be bonded must be scrupulously clean—even traces of skin oils will impair the strength of the join; care must be taken to eliminate all air bubbles from the adhesive; the glass used must be thick enough to withstand the pressure—use $\frac{1}{4}$ in (6 mm) thick glass for depths up to 10 in (25 cm) and $\frac{3}{8}$ in (9 mm) thick glass for depths up to 18 in (45 cm). The back and side walls of the tank can be painted (on the outside) with blue paint, or panelled with blue plastic, to create an impression of depth. This has the further advantage of giving the fishes a greater sense of security. The front of the tank may be similarly 'framed' to hide from view the base gravel-filter and the surface of the water. The whole base area of the tank must be supported by a sheet of blockboard or plywood of adequate thickness.

The wooden tank This unusual form of construction has the advantage of cheapness. Thick marine ply, $\frac{3}{4}$ in (9 mm) thick, is used for the base, back and ends, and the front is a wooden frame bearing the glass panel. The ply is glued together with resin and pinned. The structure should be strengthened with wooden rails and cross members at the top to prevent bowing. The interior wood should be sealed with a non-toxic epoxy or glass-fibre-reinforced polyester resin. A glass to resin bond can be effected with a synthetic rubber mastic (again surfaces must be clean). After allowing it to dry, the tank should be cured with strong salt solution for 5–7 days. A marine varnish may be applied to the outside.

This type of tank offers the greatest savings to those who require a deep tank for the culture of deep-bodied fishes such as Moorish Idols, angelfishes and butterfly-fishes.

Plastic-coated iron frame This is a conventionally constructed tank but the angle iron is coated with a plastic to prevent corrosion. It is better to buy a tank with a nylon-coated frame rather than one with a PVC or polythene coated frame. The seams should be sealed with silicone rubber—it is most unlikely that this will have been done by the manufacturer—in order to prevent toxins from the oil-based glazing putty from entering the aquarium water. This type of tank is expensive to buy.

Stainless-steel frame In the author's experience, no cheap stainless steel frame has ever proved completely rust resistant; some kind of sealing is essential.

Angle iron frame The angle-iron-framed tank has been the basis of the home aquarium for at least seventy years, but because of the extremely corrosive nature of sea water it is quite unsuitable for marine use unless the metal is first insulated from direct contact with the water. The tank should be completely stripped down, the frame sand-blasted and insulated with polyester resin and glass-fibre tissue, and the aquarium then carefully re-glazed. Thoroughly clean the inside of the tank and seal the seams with silicone rubber.

All-plastic In the smaller sizes—up to $24 \times 12 \times 12$ in $(60 \times 30 \times 30)$—these tanks are extremely good value. Their main disadvantage is that clumsy cleaning of the front panel can result in serious scratching. Against this —and it must be admitted that a scratched panel is a rebuke to the aquarist rather than the tank—must be set non-toxicity, non-corrosibility, low cost and low weight.

Hoods and covers The tank should have a well-fitting glass cover to keep dust out of the aquarium and to allow condensation and splash to run back into the water. Hoods are often made of aluminium, a metal whose toxicity to coral fishes is rivalled only by copper and zinc. An aluminium hood should be coated with a suitable primer, painted with a good white undercoat and given a gloss finish.

SEA WATER—SYNTHETIC OR NATURAL?

Natural sea water is often dirty, polluted and infected; it is always inconvenient, and therefore costly, to collect and cure; no marine organism, whether plant, fish or invertebrate, appears able to differentiate between natural and good synthetic sea water. When a marine aquarium is established enough salt is added to the water to give a hydrometer reading, when totally dissolved, of 1·018 to 1·021 (up to 1·023 for invertebrates). Until a partial water change is undertaken (after three months to three years depending on stocking and water management techniques) all that is required is to make up evaporation losses with distilled water or tap water that has been allowed to stand.

HYDROMETERS

Do not attempt to save money by buying a cheap hydrometer. A correctly made marine hydrometer will be calibrated at a temperature of about 75°F (24°C) since this is the temperature at which most aquarists keep their coral fishes. If the water temperature is too far from the calibration temperature an incorrect reading will be taken. Surface tension affects the hydrometer reading significantly: the same sea water may give different hydrometer readings before and after a heavy feed or with a dirty and a clean hydrometer.

THERMOMETERS

Again, it is wise to buy a good instrument. Thermometers are of two basic types: those which are immersed and held in place by a plastic sucker adhering to the inner face of the tank, and those which adhere to an outer wall of the tank and sense the temperature through the glass. The former type is generally much cheaper. In any event a check on the instrument's accuracy is advisable; a known and consistent error can be compensated for when taking readings.

HEATING

The safest and most convenient method of heating the water is with a combined heater and thermostat. Some of the cheaper models available are liable to burst; this is extremely dangerous in liquid like sea water which has a high electrical conductivity. Use an all-plastic holder

A mixed aquarium

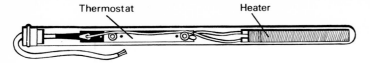

Combined heater-thermostat. Since rubber is swiftly perished by sea water the unit should have a plastic sealing bung.

to keep the heater in an upright position with the sealer cap at or clear of the water surface. These instruments are described as being fully submersible but this is tempting fate unnecessarily. The water movement in a well-filtered and properly aerated aquarium should ensure an adequately even distribution of heat. The heater must, of course, have a sufficient power output: 100 watts per 20 UK gallons (24 US gallons) is enough for a normally heated room, but 150 watts may be needed for a poorly heated or unheated room.

FILTRATION

Initially only one filter is necessary for the sea aquarium and this is the high-powered under-gravel filter. This astonishingly efficient, yet cheap and simple device is indestructible in normal use and requires the minimum of maintenance. Powerful airlifts, operated by vibrator air pumps, draw water down through the filter-gravel

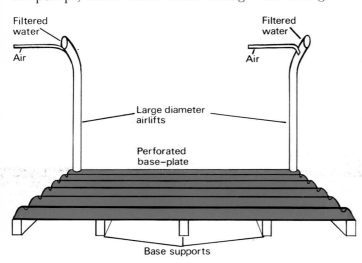

The marine under-gravel filter has large diameter airlifts to ensure a high turnover rate.

where it is purified by micro-organisms living within the filter-gravel covering a perforated plastic filter plate. Ideally this plate should cover the *total* base area of the tank.

After the aquarium has run for a while and if, owing to tank illumination inadequacies, no green algae have appeared, it is a good idea to fit a cheap plastic external or internal box filter with a *little* filter wool and a lot of high-grade marine charcoal. This prevents the build up of organic chemicals in solution which tend to discolour the sea water to such an extent that it soon assumes the tint of pale lager-type beer if not decolourized with marine charcoal. Organic pollutants at this level can be very damaging to delicate coral fishes. When the green algae appear, water discoloration is very rare.

The beginner often wonders how to tell when marine charcoal is totally de-activated. The chemical, physical and biological factors affecting charcoal in this situation are complex and inter-related. For example, an aquarist rigidly adhering to the rule: 1 in (2·5 cm) of fish to 4 UK gallons (5 US gallons) of tank space will obtain a much greater useful life from his charcoal than the one

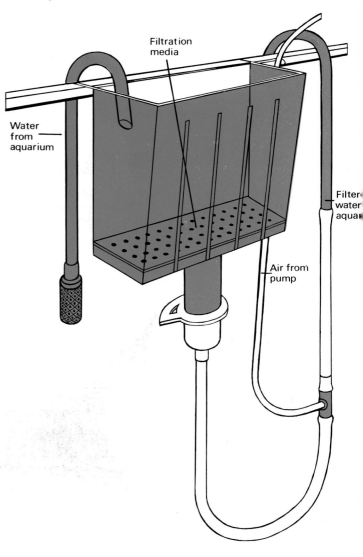

An external, air-operated filter is an inexpensive means of passing water through activated or *p*H buffering media. Water enters the filter box by siphon action and is airlifted back to the aquarium.

who overcrowds. Use the colour of the water as a guide; when the water begins to take on a brownish-yellow hue, slowly change half the activated charcoal. Too rapid a movement of the culture sea water through too much highly activated, marine grade charcoal can be more damaging to delicate marine life than the water condition which it is meant to cure.

Filtration media These are basically four in kind.

(i) *Non-calcareous gravels* Silica in its various forms, such as silver sand, beach sand, beach gravels and shingles is non-toxic and offers a wide range of colour and texture. Recently, coloured crushed and graded bottle-glass has appeared on the commercial aquatic scene and has been used in aquarium decor.

(ii) *Calcareous gravels* Crushed coral and limestone are often claimed to be *p*H buffering in effect when used in a filtration system. Owing to the chemical composition of aragonite it is indeed likely that this expected effect

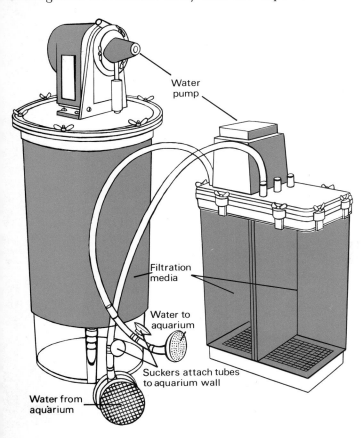

Power filters offer the high turnover rate necessary for larger marine aquaria. As with the air-operated filter, the sea water should pass through the coarser filtration media *before* reaching a filter 'wool'.

does occur. However, it would appear to have only a slight delaying effect on the inevitable depletion of the alkali reserve within sea water when it is stocked with living creatures.

(iii) *Highly activated marine charcoal* This material is expensive because it is much more highly activated than cheaper freshwater charcoals. However, it is a valuable water management aid as has been already discussed above.

(iv) *Synthetic filter 'wools'* After much work, I have almost reached the conclusion that these are only *really* useful to a marine aquarist if strongly compressed in a *power-filter*. Nonetheless, an argument of sorts could be mustered for their use in external box filters using charcoal.

Recently it has become quite fashionable to lay a layer of filter 'wool' on top of a plastic undergravel plate prior to covering it with filtrant gravel. I experimentally ran a marine tank using this method in 1967 but quickly abandoned it in the interests of hygiene. It proved impossible to clean this 'wool' pad without totally disrupting the whole aquarium. In view of the number of competent marine aquarists whom I respect who use 'wool' in this way, there must be strong arguments in its favour, but so far they have evaded me.

Air pumps There is currently such a variety of diaphragm air pumps on the market that again one must refer the inexperienced aquarist to his local aquatic trader. Needless to say, with such a large range he will find some good, some bad and many indifferent pumps on offer. The inevitable law that you always get exactly what you pay for was never truer than in this situation. Please do not waste your money on a multiplicity of small pumps—it is untidy and wasteful even though sea aquariums do need a lot of air. Conversely, do not put all your eggs in one basket and buy just a huge single-vibrator pump. Keep the air filter clean otherwise the rubber flap-valves controlling incoming and out-going air will not seat properly and will impede the correct working of the pump. Where an air-bleeder is fitted to the pump use it to reduce air pressure to an appliance rather than strangle off the appliance line with a plastic clamp. If a bleed-valve is not fitted make one by breaking the air outline line from the pump, inserting a T-piece and attaching a short length of spare air-line tube on to the T-piece's spare outlet limb. You can now control this limb with a clamp as a bleeder-device, and the life-span of the pump's rubber diaphragm will be considerably lengthened.

LIGHTING

This is as important in a marine aquarium as it is in a freshwater tank but for almost the reverse reason. A freshwater aquarist spends much time adjusting the lighting in order to encourage the higher plants used for tank decor in freshwater aquaria. As the higher plants flourish the algae die back. A marine aquarist, however, has almost no higher plants to cultivate: he carefully nurtures algae some of which look identical to those that the freshwater aquarist is so keen to destroy.

Probably the ideal balance in a coral aquarium avoiding any temperature extremes is 15–30 watts of incandescent (tungsten) light, 10 watts of colour-corrected fluorescent light and 10 watts of natural white fluorescent light per square foot of water surface. This can only be a rough guide and could be significantly modified by the proximity of the sea aquarium to a window, the number of hours per day for which each light is burnt, the depth of the water and so on.

ESTABLISHING A TROPICAL SEA AQUARIUM

The systems of running home marine aquaria can be classified roughly into three types. These are:

THE CLINICAL SYSTEM

This sort of system relies on water pump-operated *power filters*, usually filled with highly activated marine charcoal and synthetic fibre filter 'wool', for its water management. They are normally used in conjunction with another water-management aid, the *protein skimmer*.

The decay of any excess food and of matter excreted by the fishes themselves introduces harmful substances into the aquarium water. These substances may be directly toxic to the fishes; they also tend to collect as a stable foam at the surface where they act as a breeding ground for bacteria. It is the purpose of the protein skimmer to remove this material from the tank. Sea water is continually pumped into a reaction chamber where it is treated with a stream of fine air bubbles from a wooden diffuser. The unwanted organic matter is adsorbed on to the surface of the bubbles and carried to the top of the chamber. Since these bubbles are stable—contamination by the pollutant organic matter having lowered their surface tension—they remain as a scum which can be periodically removed.

Another item of advanced water-management equipment advocated by the clinician is the *ultraviolet sterilizer*. In its simplest form this is a device for circulating sea water around a source of ultraviolet radiation. Most of these units are based on the Dutch-built Philips TUV 6 lamp which consumes 6 watts of electrical energy, of which only 80 microwatts are converted into ultraviolet radiation of a sufficiently high frequency to be lethal to disease-causing bacteria and protozoa. Furthermore, since the radiation at the lethal frequency begins to diminish rather rapidly as soon as the unit is switched on—and may be practically zero after 2,000 hours—these instruments are rather expensive to maintain in a serviceable condition. For those who accept these problems gladly, the prospect of virtually bacteria- and pro-

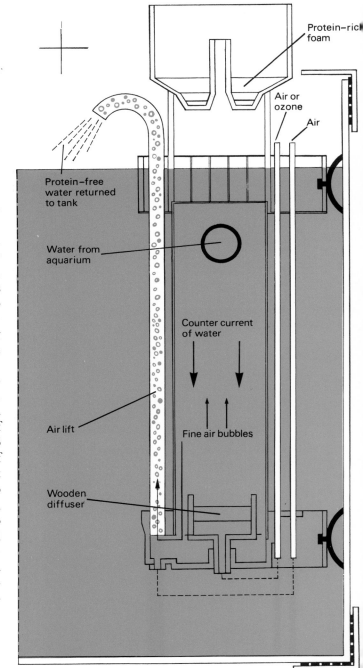

Protein-rich foam

Air or ozone

Air

Protein-free water returned to tank

Water from aquarium

Counter current of water

Air lift

Fine air bubbles

Wooden diffuser

Protein skimmer. The water level is approximately half way down a perforated plastic plate which supports the foam and prevents it from collapsing back into the reaction chamber.

tozoa-free water is a worthwhile reward. It should be stated, however, that the reduction in both quantity and variety of species of phytoplankton and zooplankton, which is the inevitable result of *effective* ultraviolet sterilization, could be detrimental to the well-being of filter-feeding invertebrates such as living corals and tube-worms.

An *ozonizer*, which may be used in conjunction with the protein skimmer, is an important item for the clinical aquarist. Ozone, an unstable triatomic form of oxygen, is a powerful oxidizing agent. This property enables it to detoxify certain waste chemicals—it converts nitrites and ammonia into harmless nitrates—and to kill bacteria. Small proportions of ozone are created from atmospheric oxygen by passing air through a strong electric field. If the tank's air supply is first ozonized in this way the water can be kept in a nearly sterile condition.

In its decor, the clinical biosystem is unmistakeable. Corals are nearly always kept in a snow-white condition as are all shells, rocks and other decor items. In the early days all manner of unnatural objects such as plastic mermaids, divers and even flowers, seemed to find their

Electricity supply

Ultraviolet lamp

Water to aquarium

Water from aquarium

Glass which transmits ultraviolet waves

Glass opaque to ultraviolet waves

Ultraviolet sterilizer. Water should be returned to the end of the tank opposite that from which it was drawn. The water may be rendered too sterile for the culture of filter-feeding invertebrates.

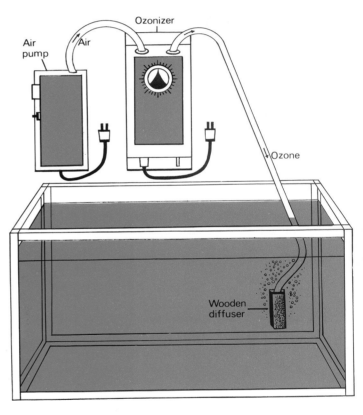

Air pump **Air** **Ozonizer**

Ozone

Wooden diffuser

Ozonizer. Since destruction of microbes depends upon physical contact with the gas it is advantageous to enlarge the surface area of ozonized air in contact with water by using a wooden diffuser.

way into the unit, and lighting was often excessively colourful; fortunately, the popularity of these items now seems to be waning. Nevertheless, some magnificent results have been and no doubt will continue to be achieved by adherents of this system. One of the finest marine aquarists anywhere in the world used this method of fish keeping and, if longevity of difficult species in captivity is any measure of success, he has a great deal to teach us all.

THE SEMI-NATURAL SYSTEM

In essence this method of keeping reef-dwelling creatures alive in captivity depends on the technical excellence and ease of maintenance of a high-powered, undergravel filter. Once understood, this superficially primitive device is a boon to the serious marine aquarist. For the vast majority of marine fish keepers the large-diameter airlift is still the finest way of moving large quantities of sea water in less time, at lower specific cost and with greater safety than any electrically operated liquid pump currently on the market. It is still my view that most intending marine aquarists who are prepared to follow well-meaning and considered advice should begin

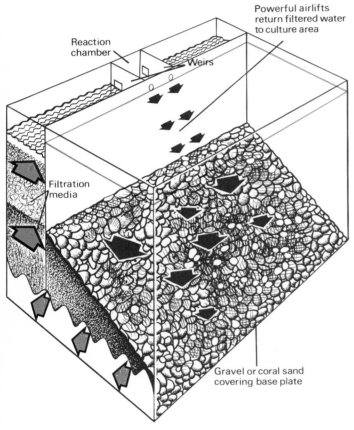

Powerful airlifts return filtered water to culture area

Reaction chamber

Weirs

Filtration media

Gravel or coral sand covering base plate

A complete marine filtration system combining the high nitrification potential of an under-gravel filter with additional filtration

the marine hobby with an undergravel filter-based semi-natural system.

Pile gravel of $\frac{1}{8}$–$\frac{1}{4}$ in (3–6 mm) mean diameter—it makes little difference whether it is calcareous or non-calcareous—on top of the perforated base plate. Ideally, this should have as many small holes as possible without resulting in the collapse of the plate under the weight of the gravel. It is equally important that the holes should not be too large, otherwise gravel will fall through them and obstruct the water flow beneath the plate. It should cover the total base area of the tank so that no unfiltered pockets of gravel are left where anaerobic decomposition of organic wastes could occur. The poisonous gases resulting from such decomposition can have lethal effects on fishes if unchecked.

The undergravel filter is operated by two small air pumps. Two are used for safety, although it is possible to use only one; it is the cheapness, durability and ease of replacement of the diaphragm in a silent, modern air pump which contributes in large measure to the superiority of the undergravel filter-based semi-natural system. The water turnover rate/cost ratio of the properly designed undergravel filter is much higher than for the power filter.

Because the water intake 'suction' is spread over the whole basal area of the aquarium the suction at any point on the gravel surface is so weak that all except the non-mobile plankton are well able to resist the pull of the filtration system. They thus remain suspended in the culture area of the biosystem where they become available to filter-feeding invertebrates.

The reader may wonder why so much attention is paid to the welfare of filter-feeding invertebrates in a book concerned principally with fishes; the reason for this is that during a recent collecting trip among the beautiful coral islands of the outer Philippines it was brought home to me very forcibly that each reef supports a balanced community of both fishes and invertebrates. The segregation into fishes *or* invertebrates which many marine fish keepers impose on their aquaria is completely foreign to the natural environment. I feel certain that in the coming years invertebrates will come more and more into their own as full contributors to a truly balanced and, therefore, beautiful sea aquarium.

THE NATURAL SYSTEM

Adherents of this method of marine aquarium maintenance attempt to reproduce in the aquarium an exact counterpart of the environment found on a coral reef in nature. They eschew all water-management aids except the air diffuser block in recognition of the fact that very few marine animals will tolerate stagnant sea water. The flow of air bubbles through the water increases the surface area of liquid in contact with the air which in turn facilitates gas exchange—mostly carbon dioxide out of, but also some oxygen into, the water. The circulating movement of the water within the aquarium also creates conditions more like those which obtain on the coral reef.

The impact of a well-stocked tank established on this principle is unforgettable. All manner of creatures thrive, impressing one with their vigour and natural behaviour. It is unfortunate that owing to the minute nitrification potential within such a biosystem great skill and/or cheap access to replacement creatures are essential qualifications for most of those who may contemplate experimentation along these lines. Although the situation is changing constantly, it is perhaps significant that despite the early publicity given to the idea by Lee Chin Eng of Indonesia in the early 1950s, and more recently by R. A. Risley's excellent book, *The Natural System* (written in Singapore), this system is really popular only in those parts of the tropics where coral reefs are to hand and marine animal prices, therefore, low.

The natural system has much to recommend it but I feel that a premature wave of popularity in the western world, with its rapidly growing consumption of reef life, could have disastrous effects on reef populations. This would very rightly bring about countermeasures by conservation-minded governments to the detriment of all marine aquarists everywhere. It is to be hoped that Mr Risley's advice and experience may soon be fully assimilated so that animals and plants are able to live out their full life spans in filterless aquaria.

It will be apparent from the above brief appraisal of the three modes of keeping coral fishes currently available that one of the author's guiding philosophies is 'Moderation in all things'. This, coupled with shortage of writing space and an unrelenting determination to reject the old and equally the new, until it has proved its worth, means that the next section will deal only with the setting-up of a tank along semi-natural lines.

CREATING A MARINE AQUARIUM

The semi-natural marine aquarium is the most satisfactory method I know of maintaining coral-reef creatures in a good state of health for long periods of time. The basic equipment needed to establish such an aquarium is: one $36 \times 18 \times 18$ in ($90 \times 45 \times 45$ cm) tank; hood; stand; undergravel filter; filtrant medium; two air pumps; air lines; air-line accessories; heater-thermostat; thermometer; both fluorescent and incandescent lighting; electrical cable and fittings; synthetic sea salt; hydrometer; nitrite test kit; pH test kit; rockwork; corals; sea-plumes (Gorgonians) and shells. By making economies wherever possible, the 1972 cost of this equipment would be in the order of £50·00 ($120). Naturally if the reader buys the very finest type of each piece of equipment listed above, the cost will be considerably greater. On the other hand, by making such equipment as the tank, hood and stand for himself, the aquarist will save considerably.

It would be possible to save money with less inconvenience by buying a smaller tank since this obviously has far-reaching effects on the cost of all other items. Unlike the situation in the marine hobby which existed as recently as three years ago, the fancier of the tropical sea aquarium can now enjoy his hobby at a cost which compares favourably with that of establishing a tropical freshwater aquarium.

ASSEMBLY OF THE EQUIPMENT

Owing to the destructive nature of sea water when in contact with unprotected fabrics and wood, it is first of all necessary to ensure that a new tank has not been damaged in transit. This is done by placing it on the stand in the position it will finally occupy and filling it with tap water. After an interval of about fifteen minutes re-examine the tank from all possible angles to make certain that there are no leaks. A plastic-coated tank will, of course, have been sealed with a seam of silicone rubber applied to all interior angles prior to test-filling the tank. If such a tank is now showing a leak, there is no short and easy way of re-sealing it. The tank must be drained, preferably by using a length of clean rubber or plastic tube to siphon it empty. The inside of the tank must be scrupulously re-cleaned and perfectly dry before

re-sealing with silicone rubber. If the instructions concerning the making of an all-glass aquarium have been carefully observed there will be no leakage problem, unless the tank has been tested on a stand with a warped base. In this case sections of the seams may have sprung apart. This is very unlikely, however, since the silicone-to-glass bond is so tough—if the glass has been properly prepared—that the base of the tank will usually fracture before any of the seams give way.

Assuming that all is now well the base-plate of the undergravel filter, which should cover the whole of the base of the aquarium, is lowered into place. Cover this first with a layer of coarse gravel of $\frac{1}{4}$ in (6 mm) mean particle diameter to a depth of approximately $\frac{1}{2}$ in (13 mm) to prevent the top layer of fine gravel from falling through the filtration slots in the base-plate of the filter. This final layer of $\frac{1}{8}$ in (3 mm) mean particle diameter gravel should be added to give a total gravel depth of some $1\frac{1}{4}$ in (4 cm) at the front of the aquarium, banking gently to $2–3\frac{1}{2}$ in (5–9 cm) at the back.

Recently, it has been possible to buy coral sand from the tropics, and this is now finding favour with many marine aquarists. It is particularly useful where detritus feeders—such as several species of sea urchins and starfishes—are to be cultured, as it has been learned from observation of these creatures in their natural state that they spend all the daylight hours slowly moving over the coral sand in relatively shallow water, continually sifting it for particles of detritus. There is no doubt that in time certain individuals within these species would learn to adapt to silica gravels of various kinds, but before this took place many would undoubtedly refuse to feed and die. Owing to the expense of coral sand it is often found that a layer $\frac{1}{2}$ in (13 mm) thick of this material spread on top of a cheaper silica gravel is a good compromise. Alternatively patches of sand may be spread here and there on the aquarium floor and used an unobtrusive method of controlling the movements of certain creatures.

When the gravel bed has been roughly contoured a sheet of plastic should be spread over the gravel surface and a clean plastic bucket placed in the centre of the sheet. Empty the bag of synthetic salt and the trace elements which it contains into the bucket and run a high-pressure hosepipe into it in order to create the maximum possible agitation. During this process carbon dioxide will be given off; this is quite normal and, indeed, necessary if the salt water is to reach the desired alkalinity (pH 7·9–8·4) depending on the quality of the water being used). If the tank in question is $36 \times 12 \times 15$ in ($90 \times 30 \times 38$ cm) or, say, $30 \times 15 \times 15$ in ($76 \times 38 \times 38$ cm)—both these sizes are of a nominal capacity of 20 Imperial gallons (25 US gallons)—then only one twenty-gallon pack of sea salt will have been purchased and by the time the tank has filled to within 4–5 in (10–13 cm) of the top, all the salt will have dissolved. The tap should now be turned off, leaving the water-level lower than will ultimately be required. In a larger tank—say to 40 UK gallons (50 US gallons) capacity—the second box of salt should be added as soon as the first has totally dissolved in the bucket, and the filling of

the tank stopped when the water-level is 6–9 in (15–23 cm) short of the top frame. The plastic sheet and bucket should now be removed.

The next step is to arrange the decor materials within the aquarium in the following order—calcareous rock-work first (Westmorland stone, limestone or Devon Black stone, for example, according to individual choice), then well-bleached corals and finally any sea-plumes or shells. Generally speaking, the aim is to re-create a small section of a tropical sea. In effect, how-ever, because of our not unreasonable desire to see the plants and creatures for which we are going to so much trouble, we usually group tall objects towards the back of the tank and often try to hide the vertical seams of the rear corners with suitably shaped rock or coral-head. Part of the back wall of the aquarium is usually left clear so that the blue- or green-painted back panel—painted, or course, on the outside—gives an impression of deep water beyond. Unless the aquarium is to hold slow-

Peacock Lionfish *(Pterois volitans)* in the typical attitude prior to striking at prey which is swallowed whole. The action proceeds faster than the human eye can follow.

moving fishes or 'lurking' species, such as groupers, apogons, sea-horses, Blue Tangs, clownfishes, gobies and lionfishes (*Pterois* species and others), for example, then the strong temptations to crowd too much decor material into too small a tank should be avoided.

The addition of the decor materials will have dis-placed sufficient water to fill the tank to the required height which, ideally, is to the lower edge of the opening of the undergravel filter airlift bend. Both airlifts must now be connected to the air pump, using a tee-piece to divide the available air between the two lifts; an under-gravel filter having two airlifts for safety should be used on tanks up to 48 in (120 cm) in length—beyond that more airlifts should be used at intervals of 2 ft (60 cm). On switching the pump on, it almost always happens that only one airlift becomes functional owing to minute differences in the depth to which the air-line is submerged within the lift. This imbalance is easily corrected by the use of a small plastic gee-clamp or needle valve used on the air-line of the over-active airlift.

Do not bother to check the specific gravity—the 'saltiness'—of the sea water at this stage. Your hydrometer will certainly give an incorrect reading, and equally certainly it will be well below the desired 1·020–1·022 (depending on the geographical origin of the species the aquarist wishes to keep). This phenomenon is always very worrying to the beginner and is caused by the fact that the salt water which leaves the mixing bucket in the early stages of filling the tank is denser (heavier) than that leaving the bucket when the tank is nearly filled and the salt almost totally dissolved. Consequently stratification occurs and it is not until the filter has been in operation for one to four hours, depending on the efficiency of the airlifts, that a thorough mixing of the water takes place. It is, therefore, advisable that no adjustments be made to the specific gravity of the sea water until the installation is completed.

Fix the thermometer in place at this point. If the aquarium has been filled with water direct from the mains supply, it will always—in Britain at least—give too low a temperature reading. The alternative, that is filling the tank with lukewarm water by mixing the domestic hot water with mains cold water, could have swiftly lethal effects on any invertebrates placed in the system as in almost all homes the hot water is stored in a copper container. Since it is clearly preferable to fill the tank with cold water the next step is to wire the combined heater-thermostat into the circuit and immerse it at the recommended angle. Although these instruments are usually advertised as being fully submersible, it is wise to take extra precautions; leaving the top $\frac{1}{4}$ in (6 mm) or so of the glass tube above water-level in no way impairs the working of the instrument.

In those countries where the modern combined heater-thermostat is unobtainable, the old-fashioned separate heater and thermostat may be used but it is essential to take great care in wrapping the electrical joint between heater and thermostat tightly and neatly with PVC insulating tape. Then smear this joint liberally with silicone rubber, having first cleaned the area with pure carbon tetrachloride. Failure to do this will sooner or later result in salt water creeping down the cables and into the joint, thus causing a short circuit. Needless to say the general health of the aquarium is not improved by several hours without aeration, filtration and heating, so several minutes devoted to following these instructions is time well spent. Generally speaking, a good heater-thermostat will be set at 75°F (24°C) but in rare instances it may be necessary to adjust the instrument according to the instructions supplied.

Fit the splash covers next; whether these are of plastic or glass it is a good idea to make a hole of 1–2 sq in (6–12 sq cm) at the front of the tank so that food can easily be introduced into the finished unit without too much dismantling. Splash covers are always necessary with a marine aquarium to protect the vulnerable lighting equipment from the ravages of salt water. They are also essential to prevent metal-contaminated salt water from running back into the tank. It is always a good idea to paint the inside of an aluminium hood when this has not been done by the manufacturer; use a primer, followed by a white undercoat and one to two coats of white gloss paint.

If the finished aquarium is to contain fishes only, then the first one or two tiny damselfishes may be added 24 hours after the installation is completed, but if the tank is for invertebrates or a natural fish-invertebrate community, one should allow at least 48 hours to elapse (and preferably more) before adding the first hardy invertebrates to the tank. To help this maturation of the sea water it is a good idea to leave the lights on 24 hours per day, but remember to switch them off about 6 hours before introducing the first creatures to the tank in order to lower the temperature to the normal level.

THE BIOSYSTEM MATURATION PERIOD

Having allowed a minimum of two days for the partial maturation of the sea water to occur, there now begins the much longer period of time which must elapse before the filtration system matures to the point when all poisonous ammonia, nitrite and excretory products from the aquarium's occupants will be oxidized safely into nitrate salts.

This process is achieved by nitrifying bacteria which coat every particle of filtrant gravel within the aquarium, and slowly increase in number as the amount of excreted matter within the aquarium increases. This maturation can be achieved in a number of ways, all of which hinge on the introduction of organic matter into the biosystem. The methods most commonly used are described below.

Without life-forms For each 20 UK gallons (25 US gallons) of sea water, a garden pea and a piece of prawn, crab or mussel (sterilized) of approximately the same size as the pea are placed in the aquarium and left to decompose. On every other day a check is made of the nitrite level present in the water by using a nitrite testing kit as directed. When the nitrite reading has fallen to zero and stayed there for five consecutive days, the system has matured bacteriologically and more delicate fishes than damsels can be introduced safely into the tank. However, the beginner must remember that as yet his skills are minimal and so he would do well to tell his dealer that his aquarium has only just come out of the nitrite period and be advised by the dealer in his choice of suitable species.

The advantage of this method is that the aquarist is not 'saddled' with a damselfish (or any other very hardy species) which he may never have really wanted in the first place; most dealers, for obvious reasons, are naturally very reluctant to buy back fishes from beginners. It also allows a breathing space for the correction of any faults which may have appeared during the running-in period of the aquarium, although many beginners find this period of several weeks' waiting a disadvantage.

With life-forms—a fish-only aquarium Basically this system works because of the fact that different species of coral fishes have differing abilities to withstand the effects of ammonia- and nitrite-poisoning. Consequently, if we accept the fact that all newly established marine biosystems will contain water with an abnormally high ammonia, and later nitrite, content, then it would appear to be commonsense to begin stocking the new sea aquarium with fishes selected from among the very hardy species. According to the volume of the culture unit being established, so there are two distinct classes of fishes which should be purchased. The owner of a small unit (up to 30 UK gallons—37½ US gallons) should only purchase one to four damselfishes, whereas for the owner of the larger tank an appropriate number of larger, hardy showfishes may be a better choice.

The following is a list of suitable fishes for culture in an all-fish aquarium. They are placed in order of diminishing hardiness but, of course, this can only be a rough generalization as individual specimens vary considerably within a species.

Damselfishes and others	Showfishes
Sergeant Major (*Abudefduf* sp.)	Royal-blue Triggerfish (*Odonus niger*)
Domino Damsel (*Dascyllus trimaculatus*)	Emerald Triggerfish (*Balistapus undulatus*)
Cloudy Damsel (*Dascyllus carneus*)	Picasso Trigger (*Rhinecanthus aculeatus*)
Pretty Damsel (*Dascyllus marginatus*)	Queen Triggerfish (*Balistes vetula*)
Electric-blue Damsel (*Pomacentrus caeruleus*)	Clown Triggerfish (*Balistoides niger*)
Saffron-blue Damsel (*Pomacentrus melanochir*)	Jigsaw Trigger (*Pseudobalistes fuscus*)
Silver Dollar (*Monodactylus* or Malayan *argenteus*) Angel	Common Dragonfish (*Pterois volitans*)
Targetfish (*Therapon jarbua*)	Russet Dragonfish (*Pterois russellii*)
Black Velvet Damsel (*Abudefduf oxyodon*)	Green Parrot Wrasse (*Thalassoma lunare*)
	Common Batfish (*Platax orbicularis*)

If the owner of a smallish tank is unable to obtain juvenile specimens of showfishes and thus decides to mature his first sea aquarium with damselfishes he should take care to purchase only very tiny specimens of each species, and also to buy only one fish of each species. Otherwise two fishes of the same species within too small a habitat will almost certainly become very quarrelsome and there is a strong possibility that the weaker specimen will eventually be worried to death. Also, unless a school of damsels is being purchased for a large tank, it is advisable to select very small fishes; a large damsel of 2–3 in (5–8 cm) will often attack any newly introduced butterflyfish or angelfish of the same size which may be introduced to the aquarium at a later date.

If a community of several fishes is being chosen for a tank holding more than 30 UK gallons (37½ US gallons) and it is intended to include a Common Batfish among them, take care that it is considerably larger than the

other species selected and preferably one of the first fishes introduced to the tank. A batfish of any species seems to rely principally on a speedy retreat as its best mode of defence and in any aquarium other than the giant tanks of the modern oceanarium, rapid flight from a determined predator is almost impossible; all too often the batfish is bullied to death.

Once the tank has been stocked with fishes of a suitable size and temperament it is necessary to make once- or twice-daily nitrite tests of the water quality. All organic matter introduced into the aquarium either as food

Picasso Triggerfish *(Rhinecanthus aculeatus)* 'yawning' and displaying its first dorsal rays and abdominal spine erect

which is eaten and then excreted, or food not eaten and not removed instantly, or as the corpse of a dead animal rotting away unnoticed—is ultimately converted into ammonia, then nitrites and finally nitrates. The first of these three compounds, ammonia, is fatal to all fishes and invertebrates, nitrites are very toxic but nitrates in moderate amounts are tolerated very well by all marine creatures. By keeping a constant vigil on the feeding situation and by giving only sufficient food to keep the fishes as healthy and active as is possible, the level of nitrite will not reach 20 parts per million (ppm).

The effects on fishes of nitrite toxins dissolved in the sea water differ in degree but not in kind. The fish becomes debilitated and almost invariably develops Velvet disease. It is not known whether the nitrites actually weaken the fish directly or are simply conducive to a population explosion of the *Oodinium* dinoflagellate parasites responsible for the disease. It is probable that the prevalence of *Oodinium* disease among fishes exposed to a high nitrite level in non-medicated water results from a combination of both factors.

The following sequence of events cannot be overstressed—it is one of the most important lessons to be learnt by the beginner.

(i) The beginner's unmatured biosystem will begin to show a nitrite reading within two to seven days of introducing living creatures; prior to this the even more dangerous ammonia content of the water will have begun to rise.

(ii) Clean, healthy fishes exposed to ammonia and nitrite toxins always develop *Oodinium* disease as a result of direct or indirect debilitation by these toxins.

(iii) If a fish is not treated for *Oodinium* disease within one hour of its introduction to a newly established aquarium and thereafter according to the manufacturer's instructions, almost all the fishes in the aquarium will die.

The following is a summary of points to remember when stocking a marine aquarium:

1. Do not exceed a stocking ratio of 1 in (2·5 cm) of fish—measured nose to tail end—to 4 UK gallons (5 US gallons) of water until you have at least six month's experience of maintaining a marine biosystem.

2. Even at the end of this apprenticeship period remember that increasing this proportion adversely by even as little as 1 in (2·5 cm) to 3 UK gallons (3¾ US gallons) of water will only be achieved successfully at the expense of frequent 'back-washing' of the filtrant gravel, partial water changes and the need to increase the rate of addition of alkaline-adjusting solutions and trace-element boosters.

3. In a fish-only aquarium *always* dose new additions to the aquarium as soon as they have recovered from the traumas of purchase, transport and introduction.

4. Remember when purchasing the first hardy fishes to mature the biosystem that every inch of fish thus purchased is one inch less of stocking-space availability.

5. Nearly all the hardy fishes commonly used for the initial stocking of a marine aquarium happen to be very territorally minded, that is they quickly take over a small area of the rockwork or a coral-head as their property and defend it vigorously against all comers. The exceptions to this rule are *Monodactylus argenteus*, *Therapon jarbua* and *Platax orbicularis*—these species thus have much to recommend them as system-maturers.

An invertebrate-only or community aquarium

This method works because most invertebrate animals of the less highly specialized varieties—some anemones, Feather-duster Worms, many of the crustaceans such as crabs, shrimps and prawns, the molluscs (cowries and scallops, for example) and the Black-spined Sea Urchin—seem able to tolerate the high nitrite content of the sea water in an unmatured marine biosystem without suffering too much damage. Thus the gross-feeders (anemones and crustaceans) as opposed to the filter-feeders (Feather-duster Worms and flame scallops), browsers (cowries and sea urchins) and detritus-feeders (some of the starfishes, sea urchins and sandworms) will contribute significantly to the excreted ammonia and nitrite content of the sea water and will consequently provide the nitrogen salts in solution necessary for the development of nitrifying bacteria in the gravel.

As previously described for the fish-only aquarium, checks should be made every so often as to the nitrite content of the sea water. When it is seen to have fallen to zero, indicating that the 'ripened' gravel bed has brought the maturation period of the filtration system to an end, then the culture of the more difficult invertebrate animals may be attempted.

It is also an amazing fact that, after the high nitrite level period is over, coral fishes may be introduced to the aquarium without the use of any *Oodinium* medication, provided that they have been first quarantined and treated for *Oodinium* disease.

Warning: it is important to remember that at present all effective *Oodinium* medicaments contain copper in some form or other. As such, they are extremely dangerous to all invertebrates; often invertebrate animals will die if introduced into an aquarium even though it has not been treated with an *Oodinium* medication for many months. As a result of this warning it will be seen that it is wisest to bleach-sterilize all gravel, corals and rocks before re-establishing a sea aquarium which has once contained fishes, and to use newly prepared sea water.

REFINEMENTS OF THE SEMI-NATURAL SYSTEM

The following is a brief list of special items of equipment which may be purchased by experimentally minded marine aquarists. None is absolutely essential, but all may prove helpful under certain conditions.

	Advantages	Disadvantages
1. Additional air pumps to operate:		
a) second airlift	Greater safety margin	
b) wooden diffuser	Increased oxygenation of water	
c) ozonizer	see 2)	
d) protein skimmer	see 3)	
2. Ozonizer	Prevents bacterial and fungal complications in wounds	Unnatural appearance of air bubbles
3. Protein skimmer	Removes surplus waste in over-stocked aquarium	Unsightly, difficult to conceal and service
4. Ultraviolet sterilizer	Destroys many pathogenic microbes	May destroy food supply of filter-feeders. Short life of ultraviolet tube
5. Electronic pH meter	Greater accuracy of pH determination	
6. Electronic colorimeter	Greater accuracy of determination of levels of ammonia, nitrite and other chemicals	

THE MARINE BIOSYSTEM

The successful maintenance of a marine biosystem requires an understanding of certain basic scientific principles. The more deeply one considers the problems of designing and running a life-support system for the more delicate creatures of the coral reef, such as living corals, certain plants, and the Moorish Idol (*Zanclus cornutus*), the deeper becomes one's involvement in fundamental physics, chemistry and biology.

PHYSICAL FACTORS

Salinity The density of sea water is greater than that of pure water—that is, the weight of a given volume of sea water is greater than that of the same volume of pure water—because it contains dissolved salts. The higher the salt concentration of the water the greater is its density; measurement of water density thus provides an indication of salinity. The density of a substance is usually expressed as its *specific gravity*—the ratio of the weight of a fixed volume of the substance to the weight of the same volume of pure water. The specific gravity can be measured simply and directly with a hydrometer. For sea water typical values of specific gravity are in the region of 1·020.

Salinity is important because it influences the exchange of salts and water which takes place between marine animals and their surroundings. Most marine fishes have body fluids which are less concentrated than the sea water in which they live. The intake of salt water through the mouth and the loss of fluid through the skin and kidney creates a tendency for the fish's body fluid to become as concentrated as the sea water.

It is obvious that the intake of sea water will raise the fish's salt content. The loss of fluid through the skin and kidney results in a net loss of water because these organs are selective barriers to the movement of salt and water: molecules of water move across them with relatively greater ease than do the molecules of salts and other substances in the body fluids. At the skin, therefore, water moves out of the fish leaving salts behind in preference to an inward movement of salts from the sea. This movement of water from a region of low solute concentration into a region of high solute concentration across a barrier which selectively restricts movement of solute is called *osmosis*. One can alternatively think of the fishes'

body fluid as having a higher concentration of water than the surrounding sea. At the kidney the restriction to salt movement is relatively less severe; the urine is nevertheless a weaker solution than the blood from which it is formed and so represents a further net loss of water. In order to balance the tendency towards increased salt concentration marine fishes have salt-secreting cells located in the gills. In effect fishes take in salt water and remove the excess salt from their body fluids.

The energy expended by the fish in maintaining the concentration of its body fluids at an appropriate level is directly related to the difference in concentration between the fish and its environment, the higher the salt concentration of sea water, the heavier the load on the salt-secreting cells. There is a limit to the ability of the fish to hold its internal environment constant and it is most important not to allow the specific gravity of the water to rise significantly above the preferred level. Most coral fishes should be kept in water of specific gravity 1·020. For fishes from the Red Sea the specific gravity should be 1·022. In either case the limits of acceptability are ± 0·002.

Any genuine deviation from acceptability is probably due to failure to make good evaporation losses or to topping up the water incorrectly. As water evaporates from the tank leaving the salts behind, the salinity, and hence the density, of the aquarium water rises. The loss should therefore be made good with pure water to bring the specific gravity back down to an acceptable level. Topping up with salt water will not work. Readings outside the preferred range may result from incorrect use of the hydrometer or from the use of a faulty hydrometer. Both the hydrometer and the sea water must be clean; the hydrometer must be calibrated at the water temperature of the aquarium; the hydrometer must be a good instrument accurate to within 0·001.

Temperature The fishes and the invertebrate inhabitants of a marine aquarium have little ability to regulate their own body temperature as mammals and birds do. They are *poikilothermic* and their body temperature tends to follow that of their environment. The rates of all metabolic processes are highly dependent upon temperature and the creatures in a particular marine environment are adapted to life within a narrow temperature range. The sea is a thermally stable environment, much less subject to temperature variation than fresh water. Typical water temperatures range from 75–78°F (24–26°C) for tropical marine species.

Lighting Correct lighting of the marine aquarium is essential to healthy plant growth. The presence of photosynthesizing algae is an important feature in the chemical cycle of the system. Algae use up carbon dioxide dissolved in the water and convert it into oxygen. They also take up nitrates from the water to build their own cellular protein, which may in turn be eaten by the animals in the aquarium.

CHEMICAL FACTORS

Oxygen All animals and many of the beneficial microbes in a marine biosystem require oxygen as a condition of life. It is essential to keep the oxygen concentration high by thorough aeration of the water in order to encourage the growth and well being of the organisms present. Flourishing plant growth and suitable lighting also help to oxygenate the tank. Organic pollutants often exert their chief effect by driving vital oxygen out of solution.

pH The acidity of the marine environment, like the temperature and oxygen concentration, is a determinant of the metabolism of micro-organisms. Too great an acidity encourages the activity of harmful anaerobic bacteria and this will ultimately affect all the inhabitants of the aquarium. In physical terms the acidity is a function of the concentration of hydrogen ions. This concentration is most conveniently expressed on the logarithmic pH scale. The pH of 7·0 obtained for distilled water is taken as neutral; a lower value is acidic while a higher one is alkaline. Natural sea water varies from pH 7·8 to pH 8·4 depending upon locality, time of day, season of year and depth. The aquarium should be kept at this slightly alkaline pH. Methods of measuring pH with indicator dyes are dealt with in the fresh water section.

Toxicity Apart from the introduction of uncured or dirty gravel, rocks, corals or shells, all organic material entering the aquarium does so as food or as living creatures which eventually die. Organic matter is decomposed by bacteria into chemically simpler compounds, some of which are extremely toxic. Nitrogenous waste (food and excreta) is rapidly attacked by certain bacteria known as *gelatine liquefiers* and converted into ammonium compounds. These are poisonous to marine life even in small quantities. *Nitrosomonas* bacteria are responsible for oxidizing ammonium compounds to nitrites—still toxic to animal life. In the next stage of the sequence *Nitrobacter* bacteria effect the further oxidation of nitrites to nitrates. Nitrates are relatively harmless and can be taken up by green plants, incorporated into proteins and eventually recycled when the plant is eaten or dies.

The detoxification of nitrogenous waste is an aerobic process—all three groups of bacteria involved require oxygen. The reactions which they bring about can be reversed by bacteria which flourish in anaerobic, acid conditions. Promotion of the activity of beneficial micro-

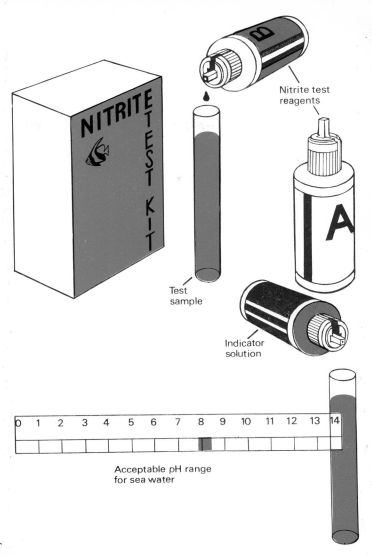

Regular testing with nitrite and pH kits indicates the suitability of the water for the maintenance of marine life and the need for partial changes of water.

organisms is essential to good water management.

In a clinical system aerobic bacteria will form colonies on the strands of filter wool and on the granulated charcoal—much of the protein waste will in any case be dealt with by the protein skimmer and never become subject to decomposition. In a natural system the bacteria colonize the available surfaces of the aquarium —walls, rocks and other objects.

STABILITY AND MATURATION

It will be evident upon consideration of what has been said already, that the integrity of a well-kept marine aquarium depends not simply on a number of separate factors acting independently but on an interaction of conditions affecting and affected by the activities of living organisms. Because temperature alters metabolic rates of activity it may also alter the levels of biological decay products and ultimately the pH and oxygen concentration. There is in any case a direct relation between oxygen tension and temperature since oxygen is less soluble in warmer water. Similarly lighting may have

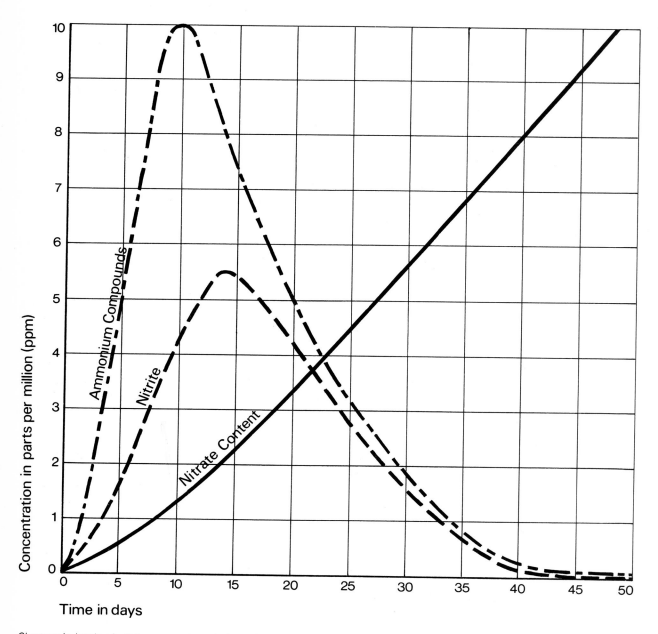

Changes in levels of nitrite, ammonia and nitrate in a newly established marine aquarium

far reaching effects through its influence on plant growth.

The delicate balance existing in a stable system is not arrived at suddenly. The accompanying graph shows the kind of changes which occur in a newly established, maturing aquarium. The time to maturity will obviously vary considerably: it may even be as rapid as 26 days if the starting conditions (stocking, feeding, filtration rate, temperature, etc.) coincide particularly well. Normally, maturation will be a matter of several weeks

and this entails some risk to the animals present in view of the high levels of ammonium and nitrite compounds obtaining in the earlier stages. Biological maturation can be speeded by maintaining fierce aeration and rapid filtration turnover, by keeping stocking and the amount of food down to a minimum, by keeping the temperature as high as the animals are accustomed to, and by stocking with hardy species.

It is above all important never to disturb the conditions in the aquarium suddenly. The effects of sharp change on such a complex balanced system are unpredictable and most likely to be harmful. Even if conditions are clearly abnormal the situation must be rectified carefully and slowly.

TYPES OF FOOD

All the food which the aquarist feeds his fishes, even if bought in some commercially prepared convenience form, is ultimately of animal or vegetable origin. Many of the flake foods offer a balanced mixture of both animal and vegetable tissues. Owing to the nitrogen content of most organic matter, food will eventually reappear in the aquarium first as ammonia, then as nitrites and will finally be converted into the less toxic nitrates. Paradoxically, therefore, all food given to your creatures is a potential source of death.

MEAT
Steak, heart and liver can all be obtained very easily from the local butcher, but please remember the minute appetites of the marine creatures in your aquarium compared with that of a human. Over-buying may result in feeding very slightly decomposed food to your fishes as you come to the tail-end of your supplies. Never give any food to your fishes and invertebrates which smells even slightly less than edible.

MARINE FOODS
The fishmonger's shop is a veritable treasure house for the aquarist. A successful foray will yield living mussels, clams, crabs, lobster and fish flesh of various kinds and these are perhaps the finest all-round foods obtainable— especially those which are still alive, such as mussels. However, it is important to remember that if the risk of infecting your fishes with marine pathogens is to be avoided, marine foods must be sterilized in a standard 'Sterazin' solution for five minutes or so and then rinsed before being introduced to the aquarium.

Prawns and shrimps, with or without their exoskeleton attached, are an excellent food. If you are lucky enough to live close to the sea, efforts will be rewarded by regular live-food collecting trips. Sand-hoppers can be collected in immense numbers on sandy shores by weighting down an old sack in the inter-tidal zone area. When the sack is retrieved after high tide it will contain an abundance of sand-hoppers and other small crustaceans trapped inside. Small soft-shelled crabs, prawns, shrimps and mussels can all be found on this region of the shore and will live for weeks in old synthetic sea water which is too 'tired' for tropical organisms.

NON-MARINE LIVE FOODS
One of the finest living foods of non-marine origin is the Brine Shrimp (*Artemia salina*). These tiny crustaceans from inland salt lakes lay eggs which, if kept dry, will remain viable for a long time. When they are added to warmed salt water and aerated they hatch in a matter of hours. They can then be siphoned through a fine strainer and, still alive, fed to the more delicate species such as angels, butterflies and filter-feeding invertebrates. Frankly, although all coral fishes love to eat these tiny delicacies, they are wasted on hardy species.

The improvement in general condition of culture animals fed on live foods rather than on a diet composed solely of prepared and flake foods is very noticeable. Live foods of non-marine origin are numerous and certainly more convenient for most fish keepers than salt-water live food. Starting with the best and most nutritious, those most commonly available are:

Earthworms These should preferably be small, very red and from wholesome soil. If this is impossible, keep them in clean moist sand for four to five days before use.

Whiteworms These small enchytrid worms are readily cultured in a peaty sand-loam. They should be fed with water-soaked bread and, if cultured carefully, breed at an astonishing rate. Their value for such 'pickers' as *Forcipiger* and *Chelmon* species (and many others of the same family) is inestimable. *All* coral fishes enjoy them, including the algae-browsing surgeons and tangs. No cleaning is necessary prior to feeding. They can survive for twelve to twenty-four hours in salt water.

Daphnia These are small crustaceans from fresh water which can often be netted in great quantities during the summer months. Owing to their size, many of the smaller, more delicate fishes appear to be afraid of them so begin cautiously by adding only two or three *Daphnia* to your aquarium at a time. They die in thirty to seventy-five seconds in salt water and their subsequent removal is almost impossible. Like Brine Shrimp, they provide excellent roughage in the diet of those fishes which will eat them.

Tubifex These are annelid worms which live in polluted fresh water. However, their unsavoury feeding habits lead to a rather suspect gut content, and they should therefore be kept in a bucket under a running tap for five to seven days prior to feeding. During this week of cleansing, frequent disturbances of the knotted mass of worms is necessary to release and wash away the excreted sewage. Once cleansed and sterilized, these worms are snapped up by even the most delicate feeders. Like *Daphnia*, they die within seconds of their introduction to salt water so never feed more than four to five worms at a time. For very timid fishes it is necessary to chop these already tiny worms with a razor blade.

VEGETABLE FOODS

In your feeding programme do not forget that although surgeons and tangs are usually considered to be the vegetation-feeding coral fishes *par excellence*, there are few species of marine fishes which will refuse *really fresh* lettuce, spinach or marine or freshwater algae. With the exception of such out and out predators as moray eels, lionfishes and the larger groupers, all coral fishes enjoy eating a little vegetable matter.

COMMERCIAL FOODS

One way of supplying this vegetation in the diet is to use green flake foods. It is a good idea, also, to experiment with some of the 'man-made' foods—freeze-dried Brine Shrimp, for example—in an effort to obtain the variety of diet which is such an essential contributory factor to the well-being of your marine creatures.

PREPARATION OF FOOD

Faced with the problem of feeding many fishes and invertebrate animals and increasingly less time in which to do it, I have found the small, metal hand-operated rotary graters available in nearly all hardware stores a very great convenience. In order to prepare several weeks' food quickly the following are necessary: space in a deep-freeze or the freezer compartment of a refrigerator; a rotary grater; basins and waste plastic cups. Deep-freeze the food until it is rock-hard, then place it in a chilled rotary grater (put the grater in the freezer for a few minutes before ready to use it), and grate the food over a basin and store it in the labelled plastic cups. By spending one hour a month preparing heart, liver, steak, prawn, mussel, earthworm, spinach, algae and lettuce in this way, the actual time spent in feeding can be vastly reduced. Furthermore, by grading the unfrozen grated food through various fish nets, particles can be obtained ranging in size from chunks suitable only for such fishes as triggers, snappers, batfishes, lionfishes and groupers, down to a finely divided 'milk' on which such invertebrate filter-feeders as crinoids, Feather-duster Worms, *Cerianthus* anemones, living corals and sponges really thrive and multiply.

Before going on to discuss techniques of fish-feeding, it would be advisable to divide the different ways in which reef creatures feed into the following categories: surface-feeders; midwater-feeders; bottom-feeders; gross-feeders; browsers; grazers; detritus-feeders; and filter-feeders. To complicate matters further, reef creatures are so adaptable that they tend not to fit neatly into an artificial scheme of classification. For example, observed in their natural habitat on the coral reef most

butterfly fishes of the *Chaetodon* genus are midwater-browsers, that is they pick and peck at tiny creatures and plants suspended in, around and actually on the living corals. In a sea aquarium, however, this behaviour may be so greatly modified that a Sunburst Butterfly Fish (*Chaetodon kleini*) may greedily snatch match head-sized chunks of prawn meat from the surface of the water, thus becoming a gross-eating surface-feeder. When the beginner has studied his aquarium for several months he will realize that there are a vast number of permutations on the theme of my eight arbitrary classifications. My advice is to use your eyes—and particularly at feeding times. Find out by observation what suits your own creatures best; keep notes, ask questions of yourself and others. Feeding—and fish keeping in general—may well be an art, but like all arts it needs an injection from science from time to time to keep it on the right lines.

GENERAL GUIDELINES TO SUCCESSFUL FEEDING

1. Variety is aptly named the spice of life and this is never truer than when applied to food choice for captive sea creatures.
2. Quantity—the golden rule is to feed very little often.
3. Match the size of food particles and the type of food offered to the species of fish being fed. Do not offer mussel milk to a Peacock Lionfish or half a squid to a Copper Band Butterfly Fish. Equally, a Powder-blue Surgeonfish will not be greatly impressed by half a lettuce.
4. Remove all food which is uneaten from the aquarium within ten minutes of the completion of feeding to avoid toxic decomposition.
5. The quality of foodstuffs can be a real problem. Sometimes this can be the fault of the fish keeper; for example, feeding partially rotten prawns because he forgot to nose-test for ammonia. Very rarely food may be toxic for reasons outside our control. Cochran (1968) records that in 1962 two Australian Navy men found some Thorny Oysters at Manus Island. Before cooking the oysters one man removed the stomach part; the second man ate the oysters whole. He died twelve hours later. In 1963 a woman from the same area died in two hours from the same poisoning. Almost all filter-feeding molluscs become poisonous at certain times of year because of dinoflagellate plankton they have eaten.
6. Stock your aquarium in such a way that you have surface-feeders, midwater-feeders and bottom-feeders. An example of such intelligent stocking in a twenty-gallon tank could be:

Surface feeder
1 small Silver Dollar (*Monodactylus argenteus*)
Midwater feeders
1 small damselfish (*Pomacentrus*, *Abudefduf* or *Dascyllus* species)
1 small surgeon or tang
1 small angel- or butterfly-fish (*Pomacanthus*, *Centropyge*, *Holacanthus*, *Chaetodon* species)
1 dwarf grouper or small wrasse
Bottom feeder
2 Philippino Scooter Blennies
Such stocking will result in a very clean aquarium.

DISEASES

Like all animals, coral fishes, and apparently to a far less extent marine invertebrates, are prone to disease. However, as a general aquarist of many years' duration, the author feels confident in saying that marine creatures in captivity are troubled far less by disease than are the denizens of the freshwater aquarium. This fact has been noted by many other workers in the field but it is fallacious to attribute this apparent freedom from trouble to the saltiness of marine water. This belief may have arisen because it was remembered that one of the earliest methods of preserving animal meat for long voyages was to pickle it in very strong brine. It is true that salt at this

concentration does impede the development of decay-producing micro-organisms, but the salinity of tropical sea water is very low. Any diver who has ever brushed a limb on a coral head and not noticed the tiny wounds until some time later will testify vividly to the fact that sea water is a rich culture medium for all sorts of pathogenic micro-organisms.

One explanation of the apparent freedom from disease of captive marine life may be that since coral fishes have always been relatively costly, right from the beginning their special requirements have been studied much more scientifically than have those of tropical freshwater fishes in the past. Do not, therefore, imagine that salt water is a magical medicinal fluid. If not properly managed it is an uncommonly rich nutrient solu-

Clownfish *(Amphiprion* sp.) suffering from white spot disease

tion in which a great multitude of pathogenic bacteria, viruses, fungi, crustaceans and protozoans will flourish just as surely as the beneficial nitrifying and de-nitrifying bacteria living in the filter-gravel.

If system management and animal husbandry are good, there will be no need for fish medicines. The importance of disease prevention cannot be stressed too often and with a knowledge of all the conditions in the aquarium which could be conducive to the outbreak of disease, and the ability to recognize them for what they are and determine the factors involved, the aquarist is well on the way to discovering how to achieve a healthy tank.

LOW OXYGEN TENSION AND/OR SEMI-STAGNANT WATER

The importance of a plentiful supply of air has already been stressed in the section on equipment. This is used for operating the under-gravel filters to create a good 'turnover-rate', that is, the number of minutes taken for the total water-content of the aquarium to pass through the base filter-gravel. This should take at least ten minutes but not longer than thirty minutes at its slowest. Such a turnover-rate will ensure that the oxygen content of the sea water passing through the gravel is always at, or near, saturation tension. This means that the nitrification potential will always be of a high order because ninety per cent of the nitrifying bacteria living in the gravel are aerobes and, once the system has matured, the ammonia excretion-nitrification process will be proceeding in dynamic equilibrium. Fierce aeration should also be used. Significant amounts of ammonia (which is relatively volatile at the high pH of healthy sea water) and carbon dioxide (released during life processes within the aquarium) will thus be forced out into the air. This is very important since both ammonia and carbon dioxide in excess are harmful to aquatic creatures. Aeration in the marine aquarium is achieved efficiently only by the use of a special wooden diffuser which produces millions of minute air-bubbles. As a result of the small diameter of these bubbles the gas is presented with a huge surface area in contact with the sea water, thus facilitating a very rapid gas exchange.

OVERCROWDING

Sometimes coral fishes die within a few hours of their introduction to a beginner's tank; very often overcrowding is one of the factors contributory to their death. Most coral fishes are very territorially-minded; within a short space of time in the new aquarium they have memorized most of its essential topographical features and especially those areas which particularly attract them. They will defend these special areas—frequently to the death—against all newcomers.

The correct procedure to adopt when introducing a new coral fish to an established aquarium is as follows:
1. Carry out the water-changing procedure for thirty to ninety minutes according to the delicacy of the species purchased.
2. Pour both water and fish into a perforated clear-plastic container, and fix the lid in position with an elastic band. Sandwich boxes drilled full of holes are ideal for this purpose.
3. Sink the sandwich box to the aquarium floor and begin normal *Oodinium* treatment of the whole tank immediately. Leave the acclimatization box on the bottom for *at least* three days and make no attempt to feed the fish in the box until the third day.
4. On the fourth day, rearrange all the rocks, shells and coral decor possible and then gently release the newcomer from the sandwich box. Within two to three minutes attempt a very light feed to detract attention even further from the new fish.

THE FISH-WATER RATIO

Always maintain a ratio of 1 in (2·5 cm) of coral fish to 4 UK gallons (5 US gallons) of water for the first six months after tank maturation, slowly increasing this to a permanent maximum of 1 in (2·5 cm) of fish to 2 UK gallons (2½ US gallons) of water. The fish measurement includes the caudal or tail fin.

A continual awareness of the natural coral reef ratio of something like 1 in (2·5 cm) of fish to 1,000 gallons of sea water will give a good idea of how like looking for a needle in a haystack it is for a pathogenic organism to find a host. Add to this the fact that on the reef the sea-water's oxygen tension is always very high, soluble proteins, ammonia, nitrite and nitrate levels are almost unreadably low, filter-feeding invertebrates are exceedingly numerous, and many pathogenic species are subjected to continual solar ultraviolet bombardment. Bearing these facts in mind, the achievement of many marine aquarists in having coral fishes live for more than three to four years in small tanks speaks very highly of their sympathetic understanding, skill and patience.

CARELESS FEEDING

It is my considered belief that of coral fishes which die prematurely in captivity, seventy-five per cent die from the direct or indirect consequences of over-feeding or malnutrition, or the sort of thoughtless stocking which does not include a bottom-feeder or a midwater scavenging damselfish or similar creature in the tank's livestock list.

POISONOUS WATER

This condition may be caused by an abnormally high content of ammonia, nitrites, nitrates, soluble proteins —'yellow-water' is quickly removed by filtration through an ultra-high-activation marine charcoal—or the accidental over-medication of captive sea water.

TRAUMATIC SHOCK

All coral fishes are rapidly debilitated by shock. If other fishes are present in the aquarium then a fish which is not fully sensible will promptly be attacked or menaced in such an unmistakable way that its condition will deteriorate quickly. Never release a new fish into an aquarium until it has recovered fully. Avoid producing a shocked fish in the first place by seeing that no rapid alteration takes place in the physical, chemical, biological or psychological environment in which it is placed.

Chaetodon triangulum showing haemorrhaged areas (red) and fin rot. Butterflyfishes in this condition rarely recover but usually die within 48 hours of the start of bleeding.

TREATMENT OF DISEASE

There now follows a treatment of the more common diseases in tabular form. Please ensure that the column headed Symptoms is studied carefully. Most investigations into claims that proprietary medications do not work reveal that the aquarist identified the nature of the disease incorrectly and thus treated the wrong disease with the wrong cure.

Disease	Symptoms	Medication	Cure period	Special notes
Oodinium	Occasionally twitching and scratching action on corals. The respiratory rate always increases to more than 100 gill-beats per minute with a corresponding increase in general listlessness and lethargy and lack of interest in food. In terminal stages the fish's body assumes a farinose appearance as its whole surface is 'peppered' with tiny parasites.	1. 'Cuprazin' or 2. Dissolve 1 gram of copper sulphate in 1 pint of distilled water. Add 20 drops to each gallon of aquarium water, having first removed all corals, shells and calcareous rockwork.	10 days at 80°F (26°C), SG 1·018 to 1·022 pH 7·9 to 8·3	This is by far the most common disease of coral fishes kept in home aquaria. It is an almost inevitable concomitant of exposure to high ammonia and nitrite levels and therefore the treatment should be maintained according to medication instructions as long as the nitrite reading persists. In addition always use 'Cuprazin' after the regular partial water-change *and* when adding new fishes.
Benedenia disease	Initially listlessness, anorexia and photophobia. After 2–3 days at 80°F (26°C) small grey-white triangular flukes appear, most densely in the eye region but eventually over the whole body surface. The apex of the triangle always points towards the fish's tail.	Exactly as for *Oodinium* disease above.	15 days at 80°F (26°C).	Benedenia appears to be most common in angel-fishes. *Pomacanthus* species are most prone—especially if exposed to nitrogenous poisoning and/or traumatic shock. The eyes are often very severely damaged and should be cared for as in *Bacterial diseases* below.
Bacterial diseases	Whitened areas around body wounds; torn finnage, opacity of cornea of eye.	1. Ozonization of sea water through fine-holed diffuser.	Until wound, lesion, etc. heals	Use continual 'background' ozonization of 5 milligrams of ozone to 20 UK gallons (25 US gallons) of water and 3 spells per day of one hour at 15 mgms/20 UK gallons.
		2. Swab the affected area with 0·1 per cent solution of acriflavine or mercurochrome	30–60 seconds	Use a very soft camelhair brush and avoid gill-contact. Place the fish on a soft, clean cloth soaked in sea water during the cure and, if possible, cover eyes and gills with the cloth.
		3. Bath in a bare hospital tank in new sea water solution containing 50 ppm of penicillin and 50 ppm of chloro-mycetin.	3–10 days. Do not attempt any feeding during the first 3 days of the bath.	As with 'Cuprazin' no charcoal filtration can be used during this cure as it removes the medication from the solution. If the fish shows signs of distress remove it immediately to an established tank. *NEVER* add antibiotics to an established aquarium.

Disease	Symptoms	Medication	Cure period	Special notes
Fungal diseases	Whitish tufty growths around the site of skin damage—usually on body, rarely on fins.	'Myxazin' according to instructions.	5–10 days at 80°F (26°C).	Turn off all charcoal filtration for the full duration of the treatment. Wash all charcoal and filter wool in clean water before re-use.
Parasitic crustacean infection.	Extreme irritation in anterior parts of the body as shown by persistent flicking, twitching of pelvic fins and scratching on decor material. *There is no increase in the respiratory rate.*	'Sterazin' according to instructions.	5 days	Turn off all charcoal filtration; precaution on re-commencement as above. Butterfly fishes, angelfishes, surgeons and tangs are most frequently parasitized by crustacea.
Pop-eye disease (Exoph-thalmus)	Eye(s) become badly swollen and stand right out of socket.	As for bacterial diseases	5 days	This disease is not caused by supersaturation of water with air as has often been suggested but by bacterial invasion of the eye tissues. A cure is often effected simply by blacking out the tank and stopping all feeding for 2 days.
White spot (*Cryptocaryon irritans*)	Pin-head sized whitish lumps irregularly distributed over body surface and finnage.	'Cuprazin'	15 days	This disease is usually caused by ammonia/nitrite intoxication. Switch off charcoal filtration.
Lymphocystis	Appearance of creamish white or pinkish cauliflower-like lumps on body and fins. No irritation or increase in gill-rate is detectable.	Surgical removal of cysts when large enough to operate.	2–5 days	Butterflies (*Chelmon* and *Forcipiger* species) and angels are most sensitive. After the removal of the cysts, the wound area must be sterilized with acriflavine or mercurochrome.
Fish-lice	Apparent to naked eye on sea-horses, pipe fishes, *Centriscus* species, cowfishes, etc.	Sterazin'	1–2 days	Turn off charcoal filtration during cure period.
Haemorr-hage	Large angry-red blotches on flanks of fish, especially butterflyfishes.	None known	None	Very rarely it is possible to save a haemorrhaging fish's life by heavy filtration, ozonization and frequent part-water changes. However, in more than 99 per cent of cases the fish should be destroyed.

CATALOGUE OF FISHES

NOTES ON THE INTRODUCTION OF NEW FISHES AND GENERAL MAINTENANCE

1. Do not buy thin fishes unless they are feeding very well.
2. Always treat newly purchased fishes with 'Cuprazin' according to the instructions. If the fish is destined for a fish-only tank it may be treated in the aquarium during its acclimatization period. If the fish is to join a community tank (an aquarium with both fishes and invertebrates) it should be treated separately in a 'hospital' tank.
3. Acclimatize a newly purchased fish in a perforated plastic box for two to three days before releasing it into an established aquarium.
4. Never attempt to feed fishes in a newly established aquarium until at least two or three days after their introduction.
5. Gradually change at least 10 per cent of the aquarium water every four to six weeks if you hope to succeed with delicate creatures.
6. Always use 'Sterazin' to sterilize any living sea-foods.
7. Continually watch the surface of the sea water for signs of incipient fouling marked by the formation of a stable foam. This indicates either overstocking or overfeeding; the former invariably leads to the latter anyway.

CLASS—CHONDRICHTHYES
Subclass—Elasmobranchi
BLUE-SPOTTED STINGRAY *Dasyatis* sp.
Grows to 15 in (38 cm); Indo-Pacific
This fish, like the closely related sharks, has cartilaginous tissue (gristle) instead of bone-tissue in its skeletal structure. It must consequently be handled very carefully when out of the water to avoid serious dislocation of the internal organs. In captivity it soon learns to accept a wide variety of live food (pea-crabs, earthworms, mussels) or fresh protein (prawn meat, crab, lobster, liver). Its coloration, behaviour and graceful movement make it highly desirable in the larger marine aquarium with large expanses of open gravel.

NURSE SHARK *Ginglymostoma cirratum*
Grows to 14 ft (4·2 m); Caribbean
Like the rays, the sharks are elasmobranchs possessing cartilaginous skeletons. This is probably the ideal shark for the sea aquarium owner since its hardiness is legendary. Like the ray above, most of its food location appears to be by scent—foodstuffs should be placed with due regard to the prevailing currents within the aquarium if they are not to be snapped up by other fishes before this rather idle creature finds them. Although the Nurse Shark may reach a length of 14 ft in nature, the common size for the home aquarium is 10–14 in (25–35 cm).

CLASS—OSTEICHTYES
Family—Holocentridae
SOLDIERFISH or SQUIRRELFISH *Holocentrus diadema*
Grows to 12 in (30 cm); Indo-Pacific
This particular species is only found in the Indo-Pacific area but the family has successfully colonized the warm seas of the world. Like nocturnal feeders it is red in colour. *Holocentrus diadema* is probably a more gorgeous red than any other salt water fish. A mid-water gross-feeder of catholic taste, it should not be trusted with smaller species unless there is adequate cover in the aquarium.

Family—Syngnathidae
SEA-HORSE *Hippocampus kuda*
Reputedly grows to 24 in (60 cm); Indo-Pacific
This species is only found in the Indo-Pacific area. Specimens are often imported in a heavily-parasitized state and, until quarantined for 14 days with 'Sterazin' treatment, they must not be placed with other fishes in a show tank. They will normally only accept small living foods such as the fry of livebearers, live Brine Shrimp, and eventually *Daphnia*. Exceptional individuals do learn to eat prawn eggs in time.

PIPEFISH *Dunckerocampus dactyliophorus*
Grows to 12 in (30 cm); Philippines
This species is found only in the Philippine area of the Pacific and is the most beautiful pipefish known. It is coloured with alternate bands of scarlet and white. Feeding is exactly as for the sea-horse above except that fish-fry are usually too large. Also, like the sea-horse, it is a midwater browser on small animal life.

Above Royal Gramma *(Gramma loreto)* with *Caulerpa* algae. If given regular algal fertilizer and subjected to strong light these plants are beneficial in removing broken down wastes from solution.

Left *Pseudochromis gutmanni*

Left Male Sea-horse *(Hippocampus kuda)* clearly showing abdominal brood pouch

Top Pipefish *(Syngnathus sp.)* swimming over *Conus* shells

Above Blowfish *(Arothron nigropunctatus)* inflated with water

Family—Centriscidae
SHRIMPFISH *Aeoliscus strigatus*
Grows to 5 in (13 cm); Indo-Pacific

For the marine aquarist who likes weird creatures and can give them a quiet community tank, the shrimpfish is a very rewarding subject for culture. Although coloration is subdued, the vertical, head-down swimming attitude of a school of six or so of these peaceful Shrimpfishes is a fascinating sight. The species is a midwater browser in habit. Feeding is as for the preceding species. Shrimpfishes are particularly susceptible to poisoning by nitrites.

Family—Theraponidae
TARGETFISH *Therapon jarbua*
Up to 12 in (30 cm); Indo-Pacific

The Targetfish is a most excellent beginner's fish. Provided that medication (as described elsewhere in this book) is used during the nitrite period, a school of six or more is very useful for maturing a large tank. In the smaller tank one or two will provide continual pleasure by their quick, intelligent movements. Their colour is bright silver with three clearly marked, black, horizontal bars. Feeding is no problem since all foods are greedily eaten.

Family—Monodactylidae
MALAYAN ANGEL or SILVER DOLLAR
Monodactylus argenteus
Grows to 5 in (13 cm); Indo-Pacific

This is another excellent species for the novice's sea aquarium. Coloration is bright platinum with two verti-

cal black bars which fade as this rapidly growing fish ages. The species is a surface and mid-water feeder on a great variety of foods both natural and prepared. In a large tank a school should be kept but in smaller tanks up to 3 ft (90 cm) long, one specimen only is best. This species (or the closely related *Monodactylus falciformis*) may occur in the Red Sea.

BAT MONO *Monodactylus sebae*
Grows to 7 in (18 cm); Eastern Atlantic

We have seen all too little of this attractive species in the past. Comments with regard to feeding are as for *Monodactylus argenteus* above, except that unless the fish has been fully quarantined after purchase, initial feeding may have to be with small, live food such as whiteworm, *Tubifex* and mosquito larvae. The body shape is much deeper than in the Malayan Angel and there are three dark brown, vertical stripes evenly spaced across the body.

Family—Tetraodontidae
GREEN FIGURE-EIGHT PUFFER *Tetradon fluviatilis*
Grows to 5 in (13 cm); Indo-Pacific

This brilliantly coloured, yellow-green puffer is normally only obtainable at 1–3 in (2–8 cm) size. Unless it is purchased in pure salt water, take at least two days slowly acclimatizing it to the marine environment. In its smaller sizes it is not usually aggressive except to members of its own species. Very few specimens learn

Grouper

to accept dried foods, but all will take whiteworms, small earthworms, small pond snails and mussel flesh with relish.

Family—Serranidae

SIX-STRIPED GROUPER *Grammistes sexlineatus*
Grows to 10 in (25 cm); Indo-Pacific
The Six-striped Grouper has six white-to-gold horizontal stripes on a near-black body. All foods are taken with voracity; tiny fishes are included unless there is plenty of cover in the aquarium *and* the grouper is regularly well fed. This is an excellent species for the owner with a large aquarium to mature and a dislike of damselfishes, monos, scats and targetfishes.

JEWEL GROUPER *Cephalopholis argus*
Grows to 14 in (35 cm); Indo-Pacific
Coloration is very similar to another grouper—*Calloplesiops altivelus*. The background colour varies from chocolate to black and the whole body is spattered with electric-blue spots, the intensity of which varies with the fish's mood. Like almost all members of the family Serranidae, the Jewel Grouper is a midwater gross-feeder favouring any form of fresh or living animal protein.

BLUE-STRIPED GROUPER *Cephalopholis boenacki*
Grows to 12 in (30 cm); Indo-Pacific
Basic body coloration is fawn with radiant, pale blue, horizontal stripes over the whole body surface including the fins. If there is such a thing as a friendly grouper, this is it. Unlike all other groupers, provided that its stomach is filled and cover is adequate, even butterflies and damsels will be ignored. A creature in captivity will seldom hunt for its food if it can obtain it more easily.

CELESTIAL GROUPER *Calloplesiops altivelus*
Grows to 8 in (20 cm); Indo-Pacific
The Celestial Grouper is one of the most spectacular of all marine creatures to become available to marine aquarists in recent years. The first to come to Europe were collected by the greatest shipper of coral fishes in the Philippines and perhaps in the world—Crescenciano Sian of A. T. Viri and Co. I received the first specimen he caught, although I know he would have dearly loved it for his own 500 gallon home aquarium. That was some seven months ago and this lovely, undemanding, gentle creature is still in perfect health. The basic colour is similar to the Jewel-spotted Grouper but overall it is so much more impressive as to hardly justify the comparison. All the usual grouper foods (prawn, crab, steak, mosquito larvae, baby guppies) are accepted with relish, but initially a marked preference for live foods is shown. During a recent collecting trip in Philippine waters a serious effort was made to find the islands where Celestial Groupers are more common, but without success. Until this area is located the species will remain expensive.

POWDER-BLUE GROUPER *Epinephelus flavocaeruleus*
Grows to 16 in (40 cm); Indo-Pacific
The coloration of this fish, both in range and tone, is almost identical to that of the totally unrelated Powder-blue Surgeonfish. It is amazing that two such different fishes should have such closely similar and exquisite colouring. Like other groupers it accepts most meaty foods greedily.

TIGER GROUPER *Promicrops lanceolatus*
Grows to 10 ft (3 m); Indo-Pacific
When juvenile, or if kept in a small tank, this species is a welcome addition to any collection of coral fishes. The bright yellow blotches on a jet-black background are not matched by any other common sea fish. It has a reputation for aggression, but adequate regular feeding will prevent it from harming other fishes. Such is the tenacity of this species that the young will enter fresh water if food becomes scarce.

PANTHERFISH *Chromileptes altivelus*
Grows to 16 in (40 cm); Indo-Pacific
This delightful creature's absurd swimming movements offset its distinctive coloration of large, round, black spots on a creamy-fawn background. Like all groupers the Pantherfish catches largish particles of food in mid-water and will feed neither off the bottom nor the surface unless it is starving to death. Even then it will often accept death as a preferable alternative to breaking with instinct.

CERISE GROUPER *Variola louti*
Grows to 30 in (75 cm); Indo-Pacific
In a family of fishes exceptional for rapid colour changes resulting from emotional flux, the Cerise Grouper is itself exceptional. A twelve-inch specimen I once owned would be quite a dull russet colour until food was intro-

Right Common Batfish *(Platax orbicularis)* attended by a Cleaner Wrasse *(Labroides dimidiatus)*. This wrasse should not be confused with the blenny, *Aspidontus taeniatus*, which mimics its shape, colour and swimming action. Larger fishes allow the approach of the mimic only to be badly bitten. The wrasse can be distinguished from its mimic by its terminal mouth in contrast to the shark like, ventral mouth of *Aspidontus*.

Below Emperor Angelfish *(Pomacanthus imperator)* showing adult coloration. The characteristic opercular spine is clearly visible.

Purple-moon Angelfish *(Pomacanthus maculosus)*

duced or until a rival Jigsaw Trigger flexed its muscles. Once thus excited, the fish went into a state I can only describe as a chromatic explosion. The body became brilliant cherry-red sprinkled with luminous blue spots. All the outer fin edges developed a daffodil-yellow border. As the nervous system returned to normal the colour would slowly subside over a 5–7 minute period. The fish is very active and strongly recommended to the beginner.

Family—Grammidae
ROYAL GRAMMA *Gramma loreto*
Grows to about 3 in (8 cm); Caribbean
Perhaps the most beautiful of the so-called dwarf groupers, the Royal Gramma has a violet frontal half with a bright yellow posterior. It presents no great culture problem to the aquarist of limited experience and feeds eagerly on all foods. Do not be worried by its abnormal swimming attitudes which vary from upside-down to head up.

BLACKCAP GRAMMA *Gramma melacara*
Grows to 4 in (10 cm); Caribbean
This common fish is rare in the sea aquarium owing to the collector's difficulties in raising it from depths of over 100 ft (30 m) in an undamaged condition. Coloration is a spectacular combination of violet-purple and black. The black area extends over the dorsal surface of the head and into the anterior sections of the dorsal fin.

Family—Pseudochromidae
DWARF YELLOW GROUPER *Pseudochromis flavescens*
Grows to 3 in (8 cm); Indo-Pacific
This is a gorgeous, little, bright yellow grouper. It is easily fed on any foods but shows a marked preference for fresh protein of animal origin. The usual grouper tendency to hide beneath rockwork and coral-heads until initial fears are overcome is clearly shown. Eventually the fish becomes one of the most showy of the tank's occupants. Like the closely related *Pseudochromis gutmanni* (Red Sea—coloration white, mauve and yellow) and the next species, the Dwarf Yellow Grouper makes an excellent addition to the smaller aquarium.

DWARF PANTHERFISH *Pseudochromis punctatus*
Grows to 3½ in (9 cm); Indo-Pacific
This species grows a little larger than some others in the genus, but it is still an excellent grouper for sea aquaria up to 3 ft (90 cm) long. The fish has a subdued coloration being almost black with off-white spots. However, despite this seemingly dull garb, its appeal is no less great than that of any of the other members of the genus. Any foods are eaten with eagerness.

Family—Apogonidae
PYJAMA CARDINAL *Apogon nematopterus*
Grows to 4 in (10 cm); Indo-Pacific
This is a small, shy fish, ideally suited to the semi-

Pyjama Cardinal *(Apogon nematopterus)*

natural community of fishes and invertebrates. The outstanding features are the well-spread fins and the many small red spots in the posterior portion of the body. Early attempts at feeding may fail unless water conditions are perfect. Small live food (*Daphnia*, Brine Shrimp, mosquito larvae, small live-bearer fry) should be offered, and the tank should be a quiet one stocked with peaceable fishes.

Family—Mullidae
CARMINE GOATFISH *Parupeneus pleurostigma*
Grows to 8 in (20 cm); Indo-Pacific

Coloration is not unlike the Cuban Hogfish, being predominantly brilliant red, yellow and white. Like all the goatfishes, specimens will jump if in a distressed condition; great care must be taken when introducing these fishes to a new environment. The Carmine Goatfish is continually scavenging the bottom of the tank for small particles of food; crustacean and mollusc flesh being preferred to all others. There are few bottom-feeding coral fishes as beautiful as this one. The brain tissue is believed to be poisonous by the people of Mozambique.

Batfish

Family—Platacidae
COMMON BATFISH *Platax orbicularis*
Grows to 30 in (75 cm); Indo-Pacific

This whole family of batfishes is presently known by three species belonging to the same genus. The Common Batfish is very easy to keep, provided that its nervous temperament is considered. All foods are greedily eaten and the growth under ideal conditions is extremely rapid. Juvenile colour is pale with 1–3 vertical brown bands, becoming increasingly darker with age.

LONGFIN BATFISH *Platax tiera*
Grows to 30 in (75 cm); Indo-Pacific

This fish is almost certainly the same species as *Tripterodon orbis* (Playfair). The juveniles are more elongate than *Platax orbicularis* and the vertical barring on the body is more pronounced. Altogether it is a more attractive fish than the preceding species, but fractionally more delicate in captivity. Occasionally small, white flecks are found on the sides, confusing beginners into thinking that the fish is diseased. Eventually it learns to take all foods but may show an early preference for earthworm and mussel.

REDFACED BATFISH *Platax pinnatus*
Grows to 24 in (60 cm); Indo-Pacific

This species is the aristocrat of the batfishes. The correct taxonomic position of the Red-face Bat is presently uncertain. The fish is always darker in colour than the preceding two species and, seen in profile from the side, it is

Longfin Batfish (*Platax teira*)

Right Rainbow Butterflyfish *(Chaetodon trifasciatus)* above, with Pearl-scale Butterflyfish *(Chaetodon chrysurus)* and Golden Butterflyfish *(Chaetodon auriga)* below

Below Three-spot Angelfish *(Holocanthus trimaculatus)*

bordered by a lovely shade of red over the marginate portions of both body and fins. Early attempts at feeding with anything other than earthworms may be unsuccessful. Tankmates are rarely tolerated.

Family—Pomacanthidae
KORAN ANGELFISH *Pomacanthus semicirculatus*
Grows to 15 in (38 cm); Indo-Pacific
Like all the Pomacanthidae, juvenile Koran Angels are quite dissimilar to adults in colour patterns. Owing to the large size reached it is usually the smaller specimens

Angelfish

that we see in the marine aquarium. They are a delightful mixture of vivid pale blue markings on a dark blue background with vertically curved white bars. All angelfishes carry a curved spine on the lower edge of the gillplate which they use in defence. By nature they are browsers in midwater but they are adaptable and soon attack all foods with eagerness.

EMPEROR ANGELFISH *Pomacanthus imperator*
Grows to 15 in (38 cm); Indo-Pacific
It is difficult to decide when this angelfish is at its most beautiful—as a vivid blue and white juvenile (it resembles the Koran Angelfish except that the white markings always fuse into a circle near the tail), or as a yellow, orange, blue, green and white adult. All the angelfishes will often grunt when annoyed but the Emperor Angel is an especially gifted performer in this respect. No difficulty should be experienced in feeding this fish since all foods are accepted.

BLUE-RING ANGELFISH *Pomacanthus annularis*
Grows to 20 in (50 cm);
The juvenile of this species bears a superficial resemblance to *Pomacanthus imperator* and *Pomacanthus semicirculatus* in that the body is bright blue with vertical bars. The bars, however, are almost perfectly straight instead of curving. The specific name *annularis* refers to a small blue circle on either side of the head just above and behind the eye. Initially feeding may be difficult for the beginner, but once started the Blue-ring Angelfish never looks back.

PURPLE-MOON ANGELFISH *Pomacanthus maculosus*
Grows to 14 in (35 cm); Red Sea
This lovely fish is one of the best suited to the owner

Koran Angelfish *(Pomacanthus semicirculatus)*

Purple-cresent Angelfish (Pomacanthus asfur) followed by juvenile
Gaterin orientalis

French Angelfish (Pomacanthus paru) showing juvenile patterning

whose aquarium has just come out of the nitrite phase. Although a little shyness may be noticed at first, it quickly learns to accept even the most mundane dried foods. Body coloration ranges from blue to blue-purple and a broad yellow crescent divides the fish in half vertically. As age increases the dorsal and anal fins elongate.

BLACK ANGELFISH *Pomacanthus arcuatus*
Grows to 18 in (45 cm); Caribbean
This species is most easily distinguishable from the next one when juvenile in that the 4–5 vertical bars on an otherwise sooty-black background are white-cream. In the French Angel they are bright yellow. Not a shy fish by any means, a good specimen will commence feeding within a few hours of becoming 'sensible' in its new home. Like all angelfishes, feeding should commence with live foods such as whiteworm, clean *Tubifex*, etc. and will progress on to all normal foods. Green flake-foods, lettuce or spinach are a valuable part of the diet of all angelfishes.

FRENCH ANGELFISH *Pomacanthus paru*
Grows to 18 in (45 cm); Caribbean
The French Angel, and its very close relative the Black Angel, both have compensations for the slow loss of the attractive vertical barring; with increasing age the tips of both the dorsal and anal fins elongate and the whole flank area develops a beautiful lattice-work pattern. This species may prove difficult to encourage to start feeding but it is very adaptable. Soaked, freeze-dried Brine Shrimp is an excellent beginning.

ROCK BEAUTY *Holocanthus tricolor*
Grows to 12 in (30 cm); Caribbean
At any size this is one of the loveliest of all the marine angelfishes. Its coloration is simple but sharp and clear. The head and lower abdominal areas are bright yellow,

whilst the rear body is blue-black. The marginate fin areas are deep orange and the region bordering the pupil is sapphire-blue. The Rock Beauty is among the toughest of all the angels—feeding seldom presents a real problem unless water conditions are less than ideal.

BLUE or QUEEN ANGELFISH *Holocanthus isabelita*
Grows to 18 in (45 cm); Caribbean
This creature goes through the same stripey juvenile phase as most other angels. At this time in its life it is blue-green, yellow and black. The species or variety known as the Queen Angelfish has a bright blue crown immediately anterior to the dorsal fin. Like all the Pomacanthidae it is a midwater browser on a great variety of foods both animal and vegetable. The latter, in the form of crushed, boiled garden peas, is greatly appreciated from time to time.

YELLOW-TAIL ANGELFISH *Holocanthus xanthurus*
Grows to 12 in (30 cm); India and Ceylon
This excellent animal is rivalled only by *Pomacanthus maculosus* as a beginner's angel. Because the body is not elongate but square, it was for a long time mistaken for a butterflyfish by those who did not notice the characteristic curved spine on the ventral edge of the gill-plate. Coloration is a pleasing mixture of pale orange, brown, yellow and black. In good conditions feeding is as easy as for damselfishes.

THREE-SPOT ANGELFISH *Holocanthus trimaculatus*
Grows to 12 in (30 cm); Indo-Pacific
If there is any colour change in this species it must occur when the fish is very small. Even 3 in (8 cm) long specimens show the full adult colour—a canary-yellow body, bright blue lips, a broad black border to the anal fin and three black spots on the head region. The species needs regular feeds of greenstuff and water quality is important. Trace elements should be artificially boosted from time to time.

Yellow-tail Angelfish *(Holocanthus xanthurus)*

MAJESTIC ANGELFISH *Euxiphipops navarchus*
Grows to 10 in (25 cm); Eastern Indo-Pacific
So far, this angelfish holds pride of place in most marine aquarists' dreams. Its main requirements are good water conditions and intelligent feeding with early emphasis on live-foods such as Brine Shrimp and whiteworm. Failing this vitamin-soaked, dried Brine Shrimp is an acceptable alternative. Its coloration is superb—a combination of orange-red, black and bright blue. Ideally, this species deserves a tank to itself and at least 6 gallons of water to one inch of overall length.

PURPLE FIREBALL *Centropyge fisheri*
Grows to 2½ in (6 cm); Indo-Pacific
This beautiful jewel is a mixture of brilliant orange and purple. As will be seen from the maximum size given, it is one of the dwarf angels and is therefore an ideal fish for the owner of a small aquarium. Feeding presents no difficulties and its longevity is prodigious. All foods are readily accepted.

ORIOLE ANGELFISH *Centropyge bicolor*
Grows to 5 in (13 cm); Pacific
Almost all fishes of this species offered in Europe originate in the Philippines. Its colour is a dramatic combination of deep royal-blue and yellow. The anterior third of the body is yellow with a blue mark around the eyes. The tail also is yellow. At first feeding should consist of small, live foods and chopped vegetable matter.

CORAL BEAUTY *Centropyge bispinosus*
Grows to 5 in (13 cm); Indo-Pacific
This is perhaps the finest dwarf angelfish for the beginner. Resistance to disease is of a high order and, under good water conditions, feeding always commences within 2–3 days. Colouring is a mixture of deep purple and russet-orange. As with all angelfishes, the first few hours in a new aquarium are accompanied by some degree of shyness, but when the fish feels ready any foods will be eagerly accepted.

LEMON-PEEL ANGELFISH *Centropyge flavissimus*
Grows to 4 in (10 cm); Central Pacific
This fish shows a distinct preference for vegetable foods. At first some spinach (frozen or natural) should be shredded very finely and offered with the minimum of commotion. If this fails and the fish is obviously hungry, then try brine shrimps. It is coloured a brilliant yellow all over with a bright blue margin to the eye, dorsal and anal fins and the edge of the gill-chamber.

CHERUB FISH *Centropyge argus*
Grows to 3 in (8 cm); Caribbean
Rivalling the Purple Fireball for sheer hardiness, this little angelfish from the other side of the world has a deep blue body and fins, with a yellow head and eyes. I have never seen a specimen as large as the maximum size quoted often. Specimens imported for sale rarely exceed 2 in (5 cm). Feeding on all foods is simple once this shy little fish becomes established.

TIBICEN ANGELFISH *Centropyge tibicen*
Grows to 4 in (10 cm); Central Pacific
The Tibicen Angel is a rather difficult subject for culture by any other than the most experienced marine aquarists. The body is black with an enamel-white blotch, situated almost centrally, and as large as the tailfin. In good specimens a faint, yellow margin is seen on the dorsal and anal fins. Feeding usually progresses from live Brine Shrimp to whiteworm to vitamin-soaked freeze-dried Brine Shrimp and other dried food.

Family—Chaetodontidae
YELLOW LONGNOSE BUTTERFLYFISH
Forcipiger longirostris
Grows to 6 in (15 cm); Pacific
The greatly elongated jaws of this species would suggest that feeding is going to be a problem. However, this is not the case and feeding often commences within a day or so provided that the fish is not badgered by a well-meaning but impatient owner. Butterflyfishes generally

Butterflyfish

feed in midwater and love to browse on rocks and corals. Rarely will it be necessary to offer live Brine Shrimp as a starter to this fish; vitamin-soaked Brine Shrimp usually suffices well. The fish is yellow with a dark head and a black spot near the tail.

COPPER-BAND BUTTERFLYFISH *Chelmon rostratus*
Grows to 5 in (13 cm); Central Pacific
This fish is a paradox with regard to feeding. Many specimens are loath to accept food in the aquarium, usually having to be tempted with small live foods. However, when a specimen dies of old age in the aquarium some three years later, its last meal would probably have consisted of dried foods. As in the previous species, the jaws are elongated. This butterfly fish is patterned with coppery-red bars on a whitish background. It bears a black spot located on the dorsal fin.

WIMPLEFISH *Heniochus acuminatus*
Grows to 12 in (30 cm); Indo-Pacific
As a juvenile, this pretty black and white striped butterfly will often display cleaning behaviour. Fishes with wounds and parasites will be approached and inspected and will allow young Wimplefishes to peck away at the affected area. One of the hardiest of all the butterflyfishes, it takes readily to aquarium life and accepts almost any food offered.

CHOCOLATE WIMPLEFISH *Heniochus varius*
Grows to 4 in (10 cm); Indo-Pacific
This wimplefish is relatively rare. Most specimens originate from the Philippines area. Coloration is dark brown with two white bars across the body converging toward the dorsal fin. As with *Pomacanthus imperator* and the next species, certain elderly specimens often have a deep indentation on the forehead. Whether this is the site of an earlier parasitic attack or the result of a natural change is unknown. Offering Brine Shrimp or whiteworm will establish the feeding habit.

RED SEA WIMPLEFISH *Heniochus intermediatus*
Grows to 10 in (25 cm); Red Sea
Although the colouring of this species is not dramatic, its hardiness and low price recommend it strongly to the owner of a large tank. Feeding is not a problem. Once established, dried foods of all types are taken. In an especially large tank several specimens will co-exist happily. Body colour is a yellow-cream with thick, dark brown stripes. The strikingly elongated first rays of the dorsal fin are characteristic of the genus.

BLACK-FACE WIMPLEFISH *Heniochus permutatus*
Grows to 8 in (20 cm); Indo-Pacific
The Black-face Wimple is a very attractive butterflyfish which is rarely seen in Europe. The head area bears a black mask, but otherwise the basic colouring is almost identical to that of *Heniochus acuminatus*. Resistance to feeding is nearly always broken by whiteworm or small *Daphnia*. Well-washed *Tubifex* will then aid the progression to dried foods. Black-faces are shy and should not be kept with other wimplefishes.

GOLDEN BUTTERFLYFISH *Chaetodon auriga*
Grows to 9 in (23 cm); Indo-Pacific
This is an all-time favourite with marine aquarists. It has won this popularity by its pretty white, black and yellow colouring, its hardiness and its catholic appetite. If such a butterflyfish goes into a decline in your aquarium then conditions are not suitable and an investigation of stocking, decor arrangement, water quality and so on should be undertaken as a matter of urgency.

BLACK-BACK BUTTERFLYFISH *Chaetodon melanotus*
Grows to 8 in (20 cm); Indo-Pacific
Whilst not as spectacularly patterned as some members of its genus, *Chaetodon melanotus* may be strongly recommended to a marine aquarist with moderate experience. Its subdued body colouring is white with parallel diagonal black stripes and the fins are yellow. *Tubifex* worms or finely chopped earthworm will start a slow

Wimplefish *(Heniochus acuminatus)* with *Caulerpa* algae in the background

Red Sea Wimplefish *(Heniochus intermedius)*

specimen feeding. These should be dropped where the fish can see them fall through the water.

BLACK-WEDGE BUTTERFLYFISH *Chaetodon falcula*
Grows to 8 in (20 cm); Indo-Pacific
The Black-wedge or Tear-drop Butterfly is all too rarely available. Its colour patterns are unpretentious in white with two black 'tears' running down a yellow-edged body. Feeding is rarely difficult, a fully sensible specimen often accepting dried foods within a matter of hours. I was once forced to place one of these fishes in a two-day old aquarium. It ate freeze-dried *Tubifex* worms the same evening.

LATTICED BUTTERFLYFISH *Chaetodon rafflesii*
Grows to 5 in (13 cm); Indo-Pacific
This butterflyfish is yellow with a criss-cross patterning of black lines. The usual dark band passes through the

Banded Butterflyfish *(Chaetodon striatus)*

eye and presumably serves to camouflage the most important end of the body. Feeding is again easy. An established member of this species will take prawn eggs, dried food and spinach.

MOON BUTTERFLYFISH *Chaetodon lunula*
Grows to 6 in (15 cm); Indo-Pacific
The colour patterning of this beautiful and hardy fish is very complex and difficult to describe. It is basically a combination of green, black and yellow. For vivacity the species rivals the Golden Butterflyfish. Because it appears to be rarer throughout its range, the Moon Butterflyfish is often the dearer. The eagerness of this butterfly to feed on any and all foods offered should not be used as an excuse for feeding one type of food exclusively. Variety in diet is a great tonic.

VAGABOND BUTTERFLYFISH *Chaetodon vagabundus*
Grows to 8 in (20 cm); Indo-Pacific
The flanks of this species have the same non-crossing

right-angle markings as *Chaetodon auriga*, and overall coloration is similar but not quite so striking. Live food such as whiteworm, *Daphnia*, small mosquito larvae or *Tubifex* is required to get most specimens feeding in the aquarium but this soon ceases to be necessary as the fish settles in.

SUNBURST BUTTERFLYFISH *Chaetodon kleini*
Grows to 6 in (15 cm); Indo-Pacific
Despite its delicate colouring—a mixture of orange, brown, purple-black and white—this fish is rarely featured in books treating aquarium fishes. The Sunburst Butterflyfish is, nevertheless, the butterflyfish *par excellence* for the beginner whose aquarium has passed the nitrite phase. Although desirable, live foods are never necessary for this species.

BROWN BUTTERFLYFISH *Chaetodon collaris*
Grows to 8 in (20 cm); India and Ceylon
Almost all specimens of this gorgeous fish which appear in aquaria are from Ceylon. Its brown-purple body with vivid white head markings and red tail are most attractive. Like nearly all midwater browsers, it prefers small moving foods until acclimatization to the aquarium environment is complete. The Brown Butterflyfish is definitely only for the advanced marine aquarist.

SADDLEBACK BUTTERFLYFISH *Chaetodon ephippium*
Grows to 10 in (25 cm); Indo-Pacific
The fact that the Saddleback Butterflyfish is rare and a bad traveller makes it an expensive purchase. Its polychromatic coloration is enhanced by a bold, black blotch with a white border located high on the rear body area. Feeding an established specimen never presents any problems, though early feedings of whiteworm help the fish to settle down.

RAINBOW BUTTERFLYFISH *Chaetodon trifasciatus*
Grows to 5 in (13 cm); Indo-Pacific
The Rainbow Butterflyfish is popularly regarded as the loveliest member of its genus; unfortunately no aquarist of my acquaintance has succeeded in keeping one alive for more than a year. In descending order of preference, early foods will be living corals, Brine Shrimp, whiteworms and *Tubifex*. With this species more than any other, it is a great mistake to allow it to become limited to any particular type of food.

ADDIS BUTTERFLYFISH *Chaetodon semilarvatus*
Grows to 8 in (20 cm); Red Sea
The astonishing durability and rich colour of this fish would make it a great aquarium favourite if smaller specimens were regularly available. The slightly diagonal, orange, parallel bars on a yellow background prevent any possibility of mistaken identity. As usual within the genus, the eye is masked by a dark coloured area. Refusal to feed for up to four weeks after purchase should not be viewed with too much alarm. Provided that all other conditions are normal, eager feeding eventually begins.

FOUR-EYED BUTTERFLYFISH *Chaetodon capistratus*
Grows to 5 in (13 cm); Caribbean
Chaetodon capistratus loves to catch a variety of living and prepared foods in midwater; once settled down in a natural habitat its feeding versatility is remarkable. The pattern of converging black stripes on a silver-white background is unusual and striking. As with all members of the genus its characteristic position of defence is head down with the dorsal fin erect.

PEARL-SCALE BUTTERFLYFISH *Chaetodon chrysurus*
Grows to 5 in (13 cm); Red Sea
This species, and the closely-related *Chaetodon mertensii* of the Indo-Pacific, are seen too infrequently in dealers' tanks. The flame-orange flash on the rear body and fins highlight a black-latticed white body. The fish is hardy, travels well, eats all before it and is not too aggressive even towards its own species if given adequate space. All butterflyfishes are very prone to shock and a great deal of thought should be given to the unpacking and introduction of these fishes into the aquarium.

Family—Acanthuridae
RED-TAILED SURGEONFISH *Acanthurus achilles*
Grows to 7 in (18 cm); Central Pacific
All my specimens of this desirable surgeonfish have originated in the Hawaiian area, though I have heard reports that the species has been sighted near Mindanao. All the surgeonfishes benefit from temporary acclimatization in a perforated plastic box in the new aquarium.

Surgeonfish/Tang

This black beauty with an elliptical red area concealing the caudal scalpel is no exception. Plenty of swimming space must always be available as these fishes are open water dwellers, only coming onto the reef for food and shelter. No food is refused and green matter should be offered whenever possible.

PYJAMA SURGEONFISH *Acanthurus lineatus*
Grows to 14 in (35 cm); Indo-Pacific
This successful fish is found over a very wide area. Differences between specimens from East Africa and from the Central Pacific can only be detected by the professional ichthyologist. Dried foods are accepted

from the outset. The body is yellow with parallel blue-green stripes.

BLUE TANG *Acanthurus coeruleus*
Grows to 14 in (35 cm); Caribbean
All the surgeonfishes and tangs are characterized by an erectile blade situated on the caudal peduncle. Normally this 'knife' is tucked away safely but, if afraid, none of the species thus equipped will hesitate to inflict deep gashes on the assailant. The Blue Tang is wonderfully coloured in the yellow juvenile phase or in the adult stage from which the species draws its name. No special feeding preferences have been noted, although algae-covered rocks and corals are appreciated.

POWDER-BLUE SURGEONFISH *Acanthurus leucosternon*
Grows to 14 in (35 cm); Caribbean
One of the aristocrats of the surgeonfish family, the Powder-blue Surgeonfish is always in great demand. It acclimatizes to aquarium life very quickly if no other surgeonfishes are present and quickly learns to take all foods.

SHOULDER TANG *Acanthurus olivaceous*
Grows to 9 in (23 cm); Indo-Pacific
The novice with a matured sea aquarium might well choose a member of this species as his first surgeonfish. Given open areas for exercise the Shoulder Tang is most undemanding. As it matures it will often be found to display a bicoloured design in which the frontal half of the body is paler than the rear half. The specific name *olivaceous* gives a good indication of the coloration. A purple-edged, orange spot occurs on the shoulder above the pectoral fin.

MAJESTIC SURGEONFISH *Acanthurus sohal*
Grows to 13 in (33 cm); Red Sea
Until recently this beautiful, hardy species was known by the specific name of *bleekeri*. Stripings on the body are like those of the Pyjama Surgeonfish but are pale blue and black. The caudal fin and scalpel are orange. When the fish is happy with its environment a bright orange 'thumb-print' occurs near the origin of the pectoral fin. All foods are accepted with relish.

EMPEROR TANG *Acanthurus xanthopterus*
Grows to 9 in (23 cm); Red Sea
With its purple round body and yellow caudal and pectoral fins, this fish is very distinctive. Feeding is very simple provided that the fish feels at home and can obtain adequate exercise. Fresh greenstuff should be given at least once weekly. More than any other species the Emperor Tang is prone to bowel constriction if inexpertly treated with copper cures. Such a condition is usually fatal.

REGAL TANG *Paracanthurus hepatus*
Grows to 6 in (15 cm); Indo-Pacific
The Regal Tang is almost like a damselfish in its eagerness to hide in corals and rockwork until certain that its

Right Magestic Angelfish *(Euxiphipops navarchus)*

Below Blue-faced Angelfish *(Euxiphipops xanthometapon)*

Left Regal Angelfish *(Pygoplites diacanthus)*

Below Yellow Longnose Butterflyfish *(Forcipiger longirostris)* with Staghorn Coral *(Acropora)* in the background. Butterflyfishes normally carry their dorsal spines erect as in this picture only when in a defensive posture. The fish will usually also adopt a head down stance when threatened.

new aquarium poses no threats which it cannot handle. Like all schooling fishes it can become aggressive toward its own spieces if too restricted for space. A strong preference is shown for well-balanced dried foods.

JAPANESE TANG *Naso lituratus*
Grows to 18 in (45 cm); Indo-Pacific
Whether common in Japanese waters or not, this species is certainly uncommon in the popular collecting areas of the Red Sea, East Africa, Ceylon and the Philippines. The body colour of the Japanese Tang is a good indication of its general state. If this is a uniform fawn-grey, all is well but if it becomes blotchy, the fish is distressed. All

Moorish Idol *(Zanclus canescens)*

Sailfin Tang *(Zebrasoma veliferum)* Red Sea-Indian Ocean variety

the fins are yellow-orange as are the scalpel and lips. This latter feature earned for the species the name of 'Lipstick Tang'. Feeding on any foodstuffs is never a problem provided that the fish is not overcrowded.

SAILFIN TANG *Zebrasoma veliferum*
Grows to 9 in (23 cm); Red Sea and Indian Ocean
The sight of a member of this species under full sail is not easily forgotten. When excited, the huge dorsal and anal fins are held fully extended and the fish swims up and down the tank in a most stately fashion. The body is patterned with vertical bars of brown, mauve, cream and black.

Family—Zanclidae
MOORISH IDOL *Zanclus canescens*
Grows to 10 in (25 cm); Indo-Pacific
After many years of studying coral fishes in the aquarium and on the reef, I have to admit that I still have problems with this fish. Nine months seems to be a very satisfactory period of culture in all except large public aquarium tanks. It would now appear that many Moorish Idols die prematurely as a result of copepod infestation. Certainly the life of a healthy specimen can

be extended by regular use of 'Sterazin'. All foods are accepted, especially vegetable-enriched dried foods.

Family—Siganidae
BADGERFISH *Lo vulpinus*
Grows to 7 in (18 cm); Central Pacific
Lo vulpinus belongs to the rabbitfish family but is far more beautiful than those usually available. The overall colour is orange-yellow but the head is strikingly marked in black and white, reminiscent of its namesake. Feeding on all foods is easy once an initial shyness is overcome.

SILVER BADGERFISH *Siganus* sp.
Grows to 8 in (20 cm); Indo-Pacific
A true rabbitfish, this species is often overlooked by those aquarists searching specifically for highly coloured creatures. The body is silver, a brown stripe passes through the eye and the head region is mottled in cobalt blue. The species is similar to *Lo vulpinus* in having a nervous disposition, but once settled in all foods are accepted, particularly green matter. Again like *Lo vulpinus* a specimen in a distressed condition will usually show a mottling of the body colour.

Family—Gobiidae
CATALINA GOBY *Lythrypnus dalli*
Grows to 1½ in (4 cm); Californian Coast
This bright red fish with five to six vertical blue bars spaced evenly across the body is one of the most gorgeous members of the family Gobiidae. This particular species has perhaps the smallest range of a wide-ranging family. It is possibly restricted to the West Coast island from which it draws its name. At first, small crustaceans such as *Artemia* and *Daphnia* may be the only food accepted, but this is a very adaptable species which will soon learn to eat most foods.

SCOOTER GOBY *Bathygobius* sp.
Grows to 3 in (8 cm); Central Pacific
Recent imports of this beautifully mottled goby have provided the marine aquarist with one of the finest

bottom-feeding browsers. Few creatures other than this cream, brown and black fish will make such a thorough job of cleaning up the base filter gravel. The pelvic fins are large and fan-like instead of being modified into a weak sucker disc as in many gobies. Nothing edible appears to be disdained.

Family—Lutianidae
ARABIAN SNAPPER *Lutianus kasmira*
Grows to 15 in (38 cm); Indo-Pacific
Body coloration is variable ranging from a pale green to a bright yellow but always with bright blue horizontal stripes. Although a midwater gross-feeder by nature,

Snapper

this snapper is so eager to feed that it quickly learns to accept food from either the owner's fingers or the bed of the aquarium. Arabian Snappers love to swim around the reef in large schools but in all except tanks of over 100 gallons only one specimen should be kept.

Spotted Sweetlips *(Gaterin* sp.)

EMPEROR SNAPPER *Lutianus sebae*
Grows to 40 in (100 cm); Indo-Pacific
As a juvenile this steep-headed snapper has three almost black stripes on a white background. However, as the fish grows rapidly under the influence of good feeding and sound water conditions the white areas become suffused with a pink shade and the once dark bars become a rich, deep red. All foods are taken avidly at the surface and in midwater but a reluctance to feed at gravel level is generally shown.

Family-Plectorhynchidae
POLKA-DOT GRUNT *Plectorhynchus chaetodonoides*
Grows to 36 in (90 cm); Indo-Pacific
The principal reason for rating this fish as a relatively difficult subject is that it rarely accepts any food in captivity other than small, live fishes. The most commonly imported size is 2–3 in (5–8 cm), baby livebearers then providing an ideal diet. Later on introduce adult Brine Shrimp, large *Daphnia* and eventually freeze-dried Brine Shrimp and earthworm.

SEA KING *Plectorhynchus orientalis*
Grows to 6 in (15 cm); Indo-Pacific
For the first few days, the Sea King may be just as demanding in its feeding requirements as the preceding species, but it very quickly adapts to all foods both live and prepared. The body is a deep chocolate brown with several oval white spots which may merge together in the abdominal region. *Plectorhynchus orientalis* is naturally a midwater gross-feeder, but may learn to feed from the surface if well cared for.

STRIPED SWEETLIPS *Gaterin lineatus*
Grows to 30 in (75 cm); Indo-Pacific
The Striped Sweetlips is easily the toughest of the three Plectorhynchidae listed here. Its colour is a rather sub-

Right Copper-band Butterflyfish *(Chelmon rostratus)*. This fish shows a lymphocystis infection in the near dorsal area. A week after this early stage the cyst will have swollen to the size of a matchhead. It can then be cut out and the area should be swabbed with acriflavine or mercurochrome.

Below *Chaetodon larvatus* with Striped Sweetlips *(Gaterin lineatus)*

dued combination of five dark brown horizontal stripes on a fawn-yellow background. The family habit of snapping up gross food particles in mid-water is well displayed, although this species' adaptability is so great that a return sweep will often result in food being taken from the bottom.

Family—Amphiprionidae
BLUE FORKTAIL DAMSELFISH *Chromis cyanae*
Grows to 5 in (13 cm); Caribbean

The damselfishes tend to live in loose 'family' groups within which there is a definite pecking order. A certain territory of rockwork or coral is defended against all-comers by each fish. The Blue Forktail is no exception to

Clownfish

this rule, although fishes of the genus *Chromis* as a whole seem to favour open water more than the species below. Colouring is blue-green with a faint dark border to the dorsal fin.

YELLOW SKUNK CLOWNFISH *Amphiprion akallopsis*
Grows to 3 in (8 cm); Indo Pacific

In this species and the closely related Pink Skunk Clown-fish (*Amphiprion perideraion*) dependence on the anemone is very pronounced. Few members of either species will stray more than a few inches away from their protecting host and even then this is only if food of any nature can be reached in no other way. Apart from an obvious difference in colour from *Amphiprion akallopsis*, *Amphiprion perideraion* has a white stripe behind the eye in addition to the white stripe which runs down the middle of the back.

FIRE CLOWNFISH *Amphiprion ephippium*
Grows to 5 in (13 cm); Central Pacific

Also called the Tomato Clown, this species is one of the toughest members of the genus. Colour seems to vary greatly from brown to brilliant red. However, all members of the species have the pure white head-band passing round the head just behind the eye. Anemones are needed in the tank if breeding attempts are to be successful, but otherwise this confident clownfish does very well just with fishes. This species accepts all foods willingly.

TEAK CLOWNFISH *Amphiprion melanopus*
Grows to 4 in (10 cm); Indo-Pacific

This fish is undistinguished in colour but very hardy. The body is an orange-brown and is divided by a white band passing behind the eye. There is some evidence to suggest that *Amphiprion melanopus* may simply represent the western race extremity of *Amphiprion ephippium* or *Amphiprion frenatus*. Dependence on the anemone is not too pronounced and all foods, including flakes, are taken.

COMMON CLOWNFISH *Amphiprion percula*
Grows to 3 in (8 cm); Pacific

All the clownfishes are characterized by their great affinity for anemones—especially of the genus *Stoichactis*, although *Discosoma* and *Radianthus* anemones will be used as temporary homes if there is no alternative. This relationship of mutual profit between anemone and fish is called *symbiosis*. The stinging tentacles of the anemones protect the fish from predators and the fish occasionally feeds and cleans the anemone. The bright orange of the body is broken up by three vivid white bands. All the fins have an attractive black border. *Amphiprion percula* will eat all foods normally offered to fishes, but shows a distinct preference for fresh protein.

SADDLEBACK CLOWNFISH *Amphiprion polymnus*
Grows to 6 in (15 cm); Central Pacific

Until recently this fish was known by the specific name of *laticlavius*. It is one of the largest of all the clownfishes and is a rather poor traveller, both factors making it an expensive fish. Once settled in it feeds very well, although chopped earthworm, mussel or squid may be necessary for the first feed. It is coloured black with a broad white band encircling the head behind the eye, a half-band or saddle across the middle of the back, and a white flash on top of the caudal fin.

BLACK CLOWNFISH *Amphiprion xanthurus*
Grows to 5 in (13 cm); Indo-Pacific

This very tough black and white clownfish with a yellow tail is now considered to be the species which was previously incorrectly identified as *Amphiprion sebae*. It has an enormous range from the mouth of the Red Sea right through the tropical Pacific. No ill effects are observed when a specimen is kept without an anemone. The Black Clownfish should be fed with fresh protein such as prawn eggs, chopped earthworm and chopped squid. Occasional feeding with a balanced dried food is much appreciated.

MAROON ANEMONEFISH *Premnas biaculeatus*
Grows to 6 in (15 cm); Central Pacific

Intra-specific aggression and aggression towards all members of the genus *Amphiprion* is exhibited by this species. Apart from the rich maroon colour and the three white vertical bars, *Premnas biaculeatus* is easily distinguished from the true clownfishes by the presence of two well-developed spines below the eye. These formidable weapons are used in threat displays and actual fighting. An anemone does not appear to be

Humbug Damselfish *(Dascyllus aruanus)*

Damselfish

essential for the Maroon Anemonefish but will often be used if present. This fish will willingly accept all foods.

PRETTY DAMSELFISH *Dascyllus marginatus*
Grows to 6 in (15 cm); Red Sea
Dascyllus marginatus always provides a welcome change from the more commonly seen damselfishes. Colouring is an indefinable mixture of chocolate-brown, fawn, white and cream and is very distinctive. A few large specimens do become aggressive, especially if they are allowed to feel that they are the most important fishes in the aquarium.

HUMBUG DAMSELFISH *Dascyllus melanurus*
Grows to 3½ in (9 cm); Indo-Pacific
The body is silvery-white with three broad, black, vertical stripes. It is very similar to *Dascyllus aruanus*—also called the Humbug Damselfish—but has a black tail, giving the impression of four vertical bands. Most specimens of the latter species originate from the Philippines. Although the damselfishes are noted for a certain pugnacity, most specimens of *Dascyllus melanurus*, if not exactly of a retiring disposition, are certainly inclined to live and let live.

DOMINO DAMSELFISH *Dascyllus trimaculatus*
Grows to 6 in (15 cm); Indo-Pacific
The Domino Damselfish is one of the more simply coloured of all coral fishes and yet it is one of the most striking. The body is generally jet-black with three small white spots about the size of the eye; two are below the centre of the dorsal fin on each side, and the remaining one is on the forehead. This is one of the fishes which the tyro may use to mature a new aquarium. Once this is accomplished, it is often necessary to encapsulate the Domino for a few days in a perforated cage while the first show fishes are added. The corals and rocks should be rearranged before the damsels are released.

Family—Abudefdufidae
BLACK VELVET DAMSELFISH *Abudefduf oxyodon*
Grows to 4½ in (11 cm); Central Pacific
This is believed by many to be the most magnificent of all the damselfishes. One should resist the temptation to

house more than one of these beauties in the same tank as they fight bitterly with their own species. Feeding is slightly difficult and live foods should be offered for the first two or three feeds.

SERGEANT MAJOR *Abudefduf saxatilis*
Grows to 6 in (15 cm); Circum-tropical
This species may almost be called the marine aquarists' guppy, so legendary is its toughness. The background colour is a pale green, with some fine dark bars crossing the body vertically. Trying to discover anything even remotely edible which this species does not eat with appreciative gusto is impossible. Since this is true of most damselfishes no further mention will be made of feeding other than exceptional requirements.

ELECTRIC-BLUE DAMSELFISH *Pomacentrus coeruleus*
Grows to 4 in (10 cm); Central Pacific
'Blue Devil' is another name for this damsel but its behaviour is no more aggressive than any other species. However, it does have a very highly developed talent for gravel excavation, using its mouth as a bucket. Once settled into a new aquarium it is not long before a small hole is dug under a rock ledge or coral head which then becomes a permanent home.

SAFFRON-BLUE DAMSELFISH *Pomacentrus melanochir*
Grows to 3½ in (9 cm); Indo-Pacific
With its radiant blue body and brilliant chrome-yellow tail, the Saffron-blue Damselfish provides an unequalled combination of colours among the lower-priced coral fishes. Again, because of intra-specific aggression, no more than one member of this species should be accommodated in tanks of less than 40 gallons unless the aquarist is certain that he can select a mated pair.

Family—Labridae
CUBAN HOGFISH *Bodianus pulchellus*
Grows to 9 in (23 cm); Caribbean
This very beautiful wrasse, coloured in red, white, yellow and black, is regrettably collected only in deep water; supplies are therefore irregular. The Cuban Hogfish adapts to aquarium life very easily and is usually taking all dried foods within a week. The colour which is prized most in this species is the brilliant red of the dorsal and ventral areas—a colour which is very rare among fishes that are active during daylight hours.

Right Japanese Tang *(Naso lituratus)*

Below Sailfin Tang *(Zebrasoma velliferum)*
Central Pacific form

Mäjestic Snapper *(Lutianus* sp.*)* with Silver
Badgerfish *(Siganus* sp.*)* at lower right

SPANISH HOGFISH *Bodianus rufus*
Grows to 24 in (60 cm); Caribbean

Although *Bodianus rufus* is not so attractive as *Bodianus pulchellus*, it is more readily available and even tougher. All of the wrasse family, to which this and the previous species belong, are great lovers of mollusc flesh. They will always appreciate a little chopped mantle or foot from a fresh mussel and this greatly improves colour and condition.

CORAL HOGFISH *Bodianus axillaris*
Grows to 8 in (20 cm); Central Pacific

Superficially the Coral Hogfish bears a pronounced resemblance to *Bodianus rufus*. In behaviour, however, it is appreciably different, being rather shy and retiring. Feeding is also a little more difficult. At first it may be necessary to offer *Tubifex*, mussel and whiteworm, but this phase rarely lasts more than a few days.

GREEN PARROT WRASSE *Thalassoma lunare*
Grows to 10 in (25 cm); Indo-Pacific

The Green Parrot Wrasse is perhaps the most forthcoming member of a family which includes some shy fishes. Although like all wrasses, it may disappear into the gravel or under a rock-ledge at night-time, during

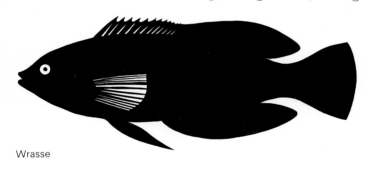

Wrasse

the day it will ostentatiously display its green, purple, yellow and blue hues to great effect. Choice of foods is never a problem with this species—rather one has difficulty in restricting feeding to that level which results in good health and sound water quality.

PURPLE QUEEN *Mirolabrichthys tuka*
Grows to 5 in (13 cm); Central Pacific

This incomparably beautiful species which is coloured deep rose-pink with a yellow throat has only very recently become available to the marine hobbyist. When I last visited the Philippines I saw for the first time a school of probably 200–300 Purple Queens. Regrettably, the remote islands where they are found are difficult to reach so that good specimens tend to be costly. I have had most success in feeding by following a progression from live Brine Shrimps through whiteworms and soaked freeze-dried Brine Shrimps to flake food.

CLEANER WRASSE *Labroides dimidiatus*
Grows to 4 in (10 cm); Indo-Pacific

The Cleaner Wrasse is a most useful member of any marine community owing to its marked fondness for removing small parasites and decaying tissue from the

bodies of other fishes. It is an amazing sight to watch a little cleaner approach a large grouper or triggerfish and clean not only the body but the area around and even inside the mouth. I have never yet seen a Cleaner Wrasse brave enough to approach a lionfish (*Pterois*) but I am sure this activity will have been recorded. This wrasse is a little nervous of new situations and care should be taken during its introduction to the aquarium.

REINDEER WRASSE *Novaculichthys taeniourus*
Grows to 12 in (30 cm); Indo-Pacific

The mottled body showing green, black, brown, cream and white together with the greatly elongated, antler-like first two rays of the dorsal fin, make this into an unmistakable species. Its special preferences are plenty of fresh protein, such as mussel and earthworm, and a good gravel bed to dive into at night. The species is not averse to biting an imprudent owner's fingers in the early days if it feels that its security is at all threatened.

BIRDMOUTH WRASSE *Gomphosus coeruleus*
Grows to 12 in (30 cm); Indo-Pacific

This curious wrasse has the elongated jaws characteristic of coral fishes which love to poke around inside coral ledges and crevices. It tends to be a midwater browser but, as we have seen when discussing *Chelmon rostratus* and *Forcipiger longirostris*, the feeding behaviour can be substantially modified by a sympathetic owner. All foods are accepted. It is not certain whether the drab brown fish known as *Gomphosus varius* is in fact the female of the dark blue *Gomphosus coeruleus* or a totally different species.

CLOWN WRASSE *Coris gaimard*
Grows to 15 in (38 cm); Indo-Pacific

Like the Cuban Hogfish, the Clown Wrasse has bright red colouring—a rare feature in diurnal species. In the juvenile phase (whose patterning bears no resemblance whatsoever to that of the adult) the dorsal outline is broken up by five black-bordered, white blotches—altogether a most distinctive livery. As with all wrasses, locomotion is achieved principally by the beating of the pectoral fins resulting in a rather curious hopping movement.

TWIN-SPOT WRASSE *Coris angulata*
Grows to 4 in (10 cm); Indo-Pacific

The Twin-spot Wrasse is only ever seen in the aquarium in its juvenile colour phase when it is a creamy white with black spotting on the head and two large, orange blotches high on the body. It is an exceptionally hardy aquarium fish which is unfortunately only irregularly available. The Twin-spot Wrasse is seldom fussy about choice of food.

Family—Callyodontidae
RED AND WHITE PARROTFISH *Bolbometapon bicolor*
Grows to 18 in (45 cm); Indo-Pacific

This species is occurring more and more regularly in shipments from the Indo-Pacific area, but so unusual is its beauty that it rarely remains in a dealer's tank for very long. The body is white with a broad red band passing through the eye. There are two red flashes in the upper and lower parts of the tailfin. A red-bordered ocellus appears in the anterior portion of the dorsal fin.

GREEN PARROTFISH *Callyodon sordidus*
Grows to 40 in (100 cm); Indo-Pacific and Red Sea
This is one of the hardiest and most beautiful of all the parrotfishes and, when obtainable in its smaller sizes, an ideal aquarium subject. All foods are taken greedily once the specimen has discovered a hiding place such as a cave or overhanging ledge. A great preference is shown for mussel flesh and crustacean meat such as prawn. Overall colouring is green, although almost every colour of the spectrum is present somewhere on the body. Parrotfishes soon learn to accept food at all depths in the aquarium.

Family—Scorpaenidae
PEACOCK LIONFISH or DRAGONFISH *Pterois volitans*
Grows to 14 in (35 cm); Indo-Pacific
In its natural habitat the lionfish is a pure predator. Mostly small fishes are taken. I once watched an adult lionfish which had trapped a school of small fishes in a coral crevice. With the huge pectoral fins outspread,

Lionfish

escape of the prey was impossible until, some five minutes later, the now bulging lionfish swam away. In the aquarium this species soon learns to accept steak, earthworm and prawn.

REGAL LIONFISH *Pterois radiata*
Grows to 10 in (25 cm); Indo-Pacific and Red Sea
This lionfish is very slow to learn to eat anything other than small, living fishes. One which I once supplied to a public aquarium learned to eat *Daphnia*, but generally the species is a little inflexible in its requirements. With its pectoral fins outstretched to display the crimson and white colouring it is a memorable sight.

Family—Echidnidae
ZEBRA MORAY EEL *Echidna zebra*
Grows to 4½ ft (1·5 m); Indo-Pacific and Red Sea

This is one of the most simply coloured and yet visually startling of all the moray eels. Its body colour is a rich purple-black, with many brilliant white vertical bars striping the body. Although the teeth of this species are not so formidable as in other morays, a large specimen will not hesitate to snap if it feels threatened. Feeding with slivers of squid flesh should be carried out in the evenings at first, although day-time feedings soon become acceptable as the newcomer settles in.

Zebra Moray Eel *(Echidna zebra)*

BLUE RIBBON EEL *Rhinomuraena* sp.
Grows to 4 ft (1·2 m); Central Pacific
Specimens of this beautiful eel have been received from the Philippines which varied in body colour from electric-blue to purple-black. Always the dorsal fin is chrome-yellow with a white border. It is not clear whether these variations represent differences in sex, geographical origin, age or species. All specimens initially need to be fed in the late evening with small, living fishes.

Family—Balistidae
ROYAL-BLUE TRIGGERFISH *Odonus niger*
Grows to 8 in (20 cm); Indo-Pacific
The Royal-blue Triggerfish is a highly desirable member of its family for inclusion in a community of coral fishes and much in demand. It is obtainable at a small

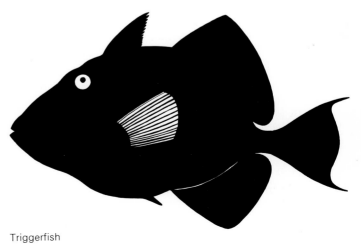

Triggerfish

Right Lilac Snapper *(Diploprion sp.)*

Below Common Clownfish *(Amphiprion percula)*

size, its colour is a lovely cobalt blue, and it is not too aggressive if well-fed. After a few days on fresh protein of any sort, all foods are accepted. If a previously docile specimen becomes aggressive it has probably outgrown the aquarium.

QUEEN TRIGGERFISH *Balistes vetula*
Grows to 20 in (50 cm); Caribbean
This lovely triggerfish is quite common in the Caribbean but single specimens have been taken on the south-east coast of Africa. The olive body is striped in dark brown and luminescent blue-green. Like all the triggers, if a specimen outgrows its environment or is inadequately fed it will probably become very aggressive.

BLACK TRIGGERFISH *Melichthys ringens*
Grows to 20 in (50 cm); Indo-Pacific
A quick examination of this fish would leave the impression that it is black all over except for white borders between the body and the dorsal and anal fins. However, a closer look reveals emerald-green stripes radiating from the eyes and many small cream markings. The enormous jaws and great distance from the eye to the mouth are adaptations to crushing crustacean shells without being blinded by snapping claws at the same time. At first it should be fed on prawn meat, but later it will accept any food.

CLOWN TRIGGERFISH *Balistoides niger*
Grows to 20 in (50 cm); Indo-Pacific
Until recently known as *Balistoides conspicillum*, this magnificent animal is undoubtedly the king of the triggerfishes. For many people it is the most desirable of all coral fishes. The Clown Triggerfish is one of the least aggressive members of its family although individual variations in temperament are bound to occur. Fresh prawn or crab meat may be necessary to initiate feeding but is not needed for long.

JIGSAW TRIGGERFISH *Pseudobalistes fuscus*
Grows to 15 in (38 cm); Red Sea and Indo-Pacific
The coloration of the Jigsaw Triggerfish varies considerably with its mood. Generally, however, it will be found to be a fawn-orange with intricate blue-green jigsaw markings spreading all over the body and fins. Bearing in mind once again the natural feeding habits of the family to which the fish belongs, prawn, crab or mussel should be offered at least once a week to supplement the more common prepared foods.

YELLOW-STRIPED EMERALD TRIGGERFISH
Balistapus undulatus
Grows to 9 in (23 cm); Red Sea and Indo-Pacific
Despite the small adult size, this species is one of the most ferocious members of the triggerfish family. Only as a 1–3 in (3–8 cm) long juvenile is it at all suitable for the small tanks of the home aquarist. A great variety of food is greedily taken at all levels in the water and growth is quite rapid. The body colour is green with parallel, curved, orange-yellow stripes, although geographical origin or mood may modify this significantly.

PICASSO TRIGGERFISH *Rhinecanthus aculeatus*
Grows to 12 in (30 cm); Indo-Pacific
The abstract colour patternings in white, black, blue and yellow on the pale cream body explain this species' common name. Frequently obtainable at the very young 1–1½ in (2–3 cm) size, a small Picasso Trigger makes an admirable member of any coral fish community. All foods are taken readily from the outset. Failure to treat this, or any newly purchased triggerfish, for *Oodinium* disease will often result in the shutting down of the more affected gill.

PINK-TAILED TRIGGERFISH *Melichthys vidua*
Grows to 15 in (38 cm); Indo-Pacific
In addition to the characteristic from which this easy-going triggerfish draws its common name, it has a distinctive blue-black body with black-bordered white dorsal and anal fins. Most specimens are retiring—even shy—and provided that the fish has adequate space, it rarely becomes aggressive. First feeds should be of prawn, mussel or earthworm, but the Pink-tailed Triggerfish will soon take flake and other dry foods.

RED SEA PICASSO FISH *Rhinecanthus assassi*
Grows to 15 in (38 cm); Red Sea
The triggerfish family, and the filefishes which follow, are all equipped with erectile spines formed from the first rays of the dorsal fin. These are used to wedge this fish firmly into crevices. Once thus locked into position, removing the triggerfish without tearing it to pieces is very difficult. *Rhinecanthus assassi* is probably the shyest of all the triggerfishes and needs sympathetic consideration of its diet and territorial requirements.

Family—Monocanthidae
ORANGE-EMERALD FILEFISH *Oxymonocanthus longirostris*
Grows to 4 in (10 cm); Indo-Pacific
Filefishes such as *Oxymonocanthus longirostris*, *Pervagor spilosoma* and *Alutera scripta* are clearly relatives of the triggerfishes and behave very much like them in all ex-

Filefish *(Monocanthus ciliatus)*

Hovercraft *(Tetrasomus gibbosus)*

cept one respect—they are very peaceful. Feeding can be difficult at first and one may have to resort to feeding live Brine Shrimp before 'weaning' the filefish on to whiteworm, *Tubifex* worms and eventually prawn eggs.

Family—Ostraciontidae
HOVERCRAFT *Tetrasomus gibbosus*
Grows to 12 in (30 cm); Indo-Pacific
This most whimsical creature not only has the shape of a miniature hovercraft, but also moves in the same apparently effortless manner by beating its nearly invisible pectoral fins. Its body is a fawn-brown colour with

Boxfish

dark brown spots. All forms of fresh protein are taken if the pieces are of the right size. Members of this species quickly learn to develop a most endearing trust in their owner.

COWFISH *Lactoria cornutus*
Grows to 18 in (45 cm); Indo-Pacific
The Cowfish, like the preceding species, is extensively covered with an armour-plated carapace. In addition it has two pairs of sharp horns, one pointing forward from above the eyes and the other rearward from below the tail. The background body colour is yellow with dark

brown mottling and numerous luminescent blue spots. Eyesight appears to be poor and it is often necessary to place small pieces of flesh before the fish's mouth for the first few days.

SPANGLED BOXFISH *Ostracion lentiginosum*
Grows to 10 in (25 cm); Red Sea and Indo-Pacific
This is perhaps the most beautifully coloured of all the boxfishes. The body is a rich, blue-black colour and is covered by many tiny white, pale green or pale blue spots. There is some evidence to suggest that some of the boxfishes may release a virulent toxin from the mouth area if in a distressed condition. None of the above three species has been suspected of this action. At first, feeding should be with Brine Shrimp, *Daphnia* or small mosquito larvae, but the species soon moves on to prawn, squid, earthworm and, eventually, dried food.

Family—Diodontidae
PORCUPINE FISH *Diodon hystrix*
Grows to 36 in (90 cm); Indo-Pacific
This member of the globefish or pufferfish family is one of the best suited species for aquarium life. The body is covered in sharp spines and is yellowish with velvety-brown blotches sprinkled on the dorsal surface. Should the fish be removed from the water or otherwise alarmed it begins to swallow air or water until its body is inflated into a spine-covered sphere. Do not be deceived by the huge, green-tinted eyes. Eyesight is poor and to start a shy specimen feeding it is often necessary to proffer chunks of mussel, squid or worm right up to the animal's mouth.

Family—Canthigasteridae
DIAMOND-FLECKED PUFFER *Canthigaster margaritatus*
Grows to 5 in (13 cm); Red Sea and Pacific
Once it acclimatizes itself to aquarium life, this easily available pufferfish is virtually indestructible. Its back-

Right Cuban Hogfish *(Bodianus pulchellus)*

Below Green Parrot Wrasse *(Thalassoma lunare)*

Left Juvenile form of Clown Wrasse
(Coris gaimard)

Below Twin-spot Wrasse (Coris angulata) about to dive into the gravel. This mode of escape from danger is possibly unique to the wrasse family.

Porcupine Fish *(Diodon hystrix)*. The upper fish is inflated in a defensive state.

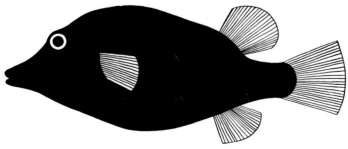

Pufferfish

ground colour is a warm brown with light blue or light green flecking and a cream abdominal region. These are quite noisy fishes and when removed from the water positively excel themselves with angry grunting sounds. Dried foods are accepted within hours of introduction to a satisfactory environment.

MINSTREL PUFFERFISH *Canthigaster valentini*
Grows to 8 in (20 cm); Indo-Pacific
The Minstrel Pufferfish appears to be uncommon everywhere throughout its vast range. It has certainly never been received in large numbers from any collecting area known to the author.

The abdomen and flanks are creamy-white in colour while the dorsal area is broken up by four black 'saddles'. As in all the puffers the jaws are rather elongate, indicating a certain choosiness with regard to food. At first a preference is shown for small moving aquatic creatures such as mosquito larvae, *Daphnia* and Brine Shrimps, but the Minstrel Pufferfish soon moves on to freeze-dried shrimp, prawn eggs and eventually dried food.

INVERTEBRATES AND PLANTS FOR THE MARINE AQUARIUM

Invertebrates are animals without a backbone or vertebral column. In the following section, several invertebrate species suitable for aquarium culture will be considered. They will be classified according to their ability to survive a high nitrite level in an unmatured tank.

When considering the establishment of a mixed invertebrate and fish community aquarium, the owner would be well advised to avoid all *Oodinium* cures. If a tank of fishes has previously been treated with an *Oodinium* cure, it would be unwise to add any invertebrate life other than hardy crustaceans.

In the author's experience the only satisfactory way to establish a coral fish-invertebrate community is to use nitrite tolerant invertebrates to mature the tank's filtration system until no nitrite reading shows, and then to add 'Cuprazin' and 'Sterazin' quarantined fishes to the system. Should any signs of skin irritation appear once the community is established then 'Sterazin' may be used provided that no crustaceans are present.

COELENTERATES

The toughest of all the tube-bodied animals are the anemones and perhaps the hardiest attractive member of this group is *Radianthus* (nitrite tolerant). This is a small anemone with an oval disc rarely exceeding 6 in (15 cm) in diameter covered with concentric circles of $\frac{1}{2}$–1 in (1–2 cm) long, pink-tipped tentacles. *Radianthus* loves to burrow its tubular body into the gravel, but will occasionally site itself on a rock. All forms of fresh protein are snatched up by the outer fringe of tentacles and swiftly conveyed to the mouth at the centre of the oval disc. In the absence of rock anemones such as *Discosoma*, *Anemonia*, or—ideally—the minute-tentacled *Stoichactis* (all non-tolerant of nitrite), clownfishes will happily associate with *Radianthus*. All the invertebrates suitable for culture in the sea aquarium require regular additions of vitamins to their foodstuffs or directly to the aquarium water.

One anemone which is not really suitable for the community sea aquarium is *Cerianthus* (nitrite tolerant). These coelenterates are often mistaken for tube-worms owing to their habit of living with the body buried in mud or sand with only the oral disc showing. There is a clear differentiation in both form and function of the tentacles of *Cerianthus*. Surrounding the large mouth is a fringe of small tentacles, surrounded in turn by many very elongated tentacles which wave gracefully in the water. The stinging powers of the *nematocysts* ('poison darts'), which are characteristic of the phylum Coelenterata, probably reach their highest development in the Ceriantharia. Even large 4–5 in (10–13 cm) long fishes will be captured by the long outer tentacles and quickly paralysed. The victim is then passed to the inner fringe of small tentacles and forced by these into the mouth. It is thus obvious that these anemones should be kept in aquaria devoted to invertebrates only. Even then they should be sited well away from all other animals.

Living corals are also coelenterates and may be regarded as miniature, colonial anemones. One important difference, however, is that coral polyps are able to extract salts from sea-water (mostly calcium carbonate) and secrete them around the outside of the body to form a limey exoskeleton. The secretions from adjacent polyps slowly fuse together to form coral heads and ultimately vast structures like the Great Barrier Reef. *Goniopora* (nitrite intolerant) corals are probably the hardiest subjects for aquarium culture. They must be given clear, colourless water and as much light as possible. The inevitable decline of *Goniopora* and other corals when poorly illuminated is probably due to the light requirements of symbiotic zooxanthellae algae living within the tissues of the polyp. In any event, with the possible exception of *Tubastrea aurea* (nitrite intolerant), a beautiful golden-yellow coral which grows under sheltering ledges, other corals I have kept have done badly unless well lit. Corals of the family Fungiidae are roughly circular with radiating divisions. They all resemble a mushroom viewed from below. Thus the scientific name of *Fungia actiniformis* (nitrite intolerant), one of the hardiest types, is not surprising. Feeding should be done on alternate evenings using living Brine Shrimps and the fluid resulting from pulverized mussel-flesh.

ANNELIDS

Polychaete worms in the marine aquarium are best represented by the Feather-duster Worm, *Sabellastarte indica*, (nitrite tolerant) of the family Sabellidae. This

Lionfish *(Pterois* or *Dendrochirus* sp.)

creature secretes a papery tube around its body. When feeding, beautifully coloured, feathery tentacles emerge from the mouth of the tube and filter planktonic organisms from the water. No feeding is necessary in the aquarium and breeding often occurs.

ECHINODERMS

Echinoderms are mostly detritus feeders or browsers; they move slowly over gravel, sand, rocks and corals, eating detritus and probably small animals and plants as well. *Protoreaster nodosus* (nitrite tolerant) from the Central Pacific area is one of the few starfishes which adapts well to aquarium life. It is a very efficient scavenger and will tackle anything from small pieces of prawn or mussel up to a 1 in (2 cm) long dead fish.

Brittlestar

Colouring is very simple, the background being a reddish-fawn with numerous dark brown nodules on the upper surface. The Black-spined Sea Urchin (*Centrechinus*) does extremely well in the aquarium, but is intolerant of nitrite. Match-head sized pieces of prawn or mussel dropped into the spines are slowly manoeuvred round to the 'jaws' (Aristotle's lantern) on the ventral side of the spine-covered test. *Prionocidaris bispinosa*, a small urchin with mauve and white-banded spines, and the pencil-spined urchins should be avoided by all except those with large fallow tanks as they appear to be specialist detritus feeders. They are in any case nitrite intolerant.

MOLLUSCS

Molluscs are soft-bodied creatures which secrete a calcareous protective shell (or shells in the case of bivalves) from special cells in the mantle tissue. Probably the best sea-snail for the beginner is the univalve *Cypraea arabica*, a cowrie which is primarily a herbivore, grazing on green and brown algae. It will, however, eat waste animal tissue and, rather disconcertingly, is very fond of eating live *Stoichactis* anemones. It is nitrite tolerant. One of the hardiest and most beautiful of the bivalves are the flame scallops (*Lima*), which are able to move rapidly through the water by clapping the two halves of the shell together. The flame scallops are filter-feeders and should receive nutrition in the same manner as

living corals. They are not tolerant of high nitrite levels.

Nudibranchs are sea-snails in which the shell has almost disappeared within the body. Some are algae-eaters whilst others eat the tentacles of anemones. None of the species I have observed has survived for more than eight weeks.

The octopus is one of the most demanding of all marine creatures in the sea-aquarium, and certainly the most intelligent of all the invertebrates. There is no tolerance of ammonia, nitrites or phenols and even nitrates in excess of 20–30 ppm may prove swiftly fatal. Once the nervous octopus has been successfully acclimatized, however, (a feat which involves perfect water conditions, good filtration and aeration, adequate places for concealment, avoidance of photo-shock) it settles down quickly and accepts aquarium life very well. A distinct preference is shown for crustacean flesh—crab, lobster or prawn meat—which must be absolutely fresh and odourless. Small fishes and crustaceans would never be safe sharing the same tank with an octopus, but other invertebrates do not seem to be molested. Rapid changes in colour and patterning as a result of emotional stimuli are a notable feature of these fascinating creatures.

CRUSTACEANS

Crustaceans include crabs, shrimps, prawns, lobsters and crayfish.

The Boxing Shrimp (*Stenopus hispidus*) is a great favourite with lovers of invertebrates owing to its non-aggressive nature (except towards its own species) and its red and white striped body and limbs. All foods are accepted willingly and certain specimens appear to clean the wounds and infected areas of fishes in much the same way as the Cleaner Wrasse. A good-sized rock cave should be provided to make these creatures feel secure. The Boxing Shrimp is nitrite tolerant.

I am often approached by beginners in a state of deep depression who inform me that the *Stenopus*, or lobster or crab which they had recently purchased is now dead. In most cases it subsequently transpires that the crustacean, having outgrown its chitinous exoskeleton, has shed it. These discarded body coverings are perfect replicas in every detail of the original owner, which will usually reappear 2–3 days later with its new exoskeleton hardened and safe.

The hermit crab (*Clibanarius*) is a very entertaining and efficient scavenger. The family Paguridae to which all the hermit crabs belong, is characterized by the lack of exoskeletal protection on the abdomen. To protect this portion of its body the crab must tuck it into the empty shell of a univalve mollusc. The mollusc shell is then dragged around by the crab until it is outgrown and quickly exchanged for a larger model. All foods are scavenged from the base of the aquarium, but at least three times per week small choice pieces of fresh protein should be offered specifically to the crab on the end of a knitting needle. Hermit crabs are not tolerant of nitrite.

MARINE PLANTS

Many new converts to the marine aquarium complain that their tanks lack the verdant beauty of the well-

Above Caribbean spiny lobster with *Chaetodon striatus*

Below Hermit crab carrying symbiotic anemones on its shell

planted freshwater aquarium. Although it is true that none of the higher plants do well in sea-water, there are several species of green, brown and red algae which thrive in a properly regulated marine biosystem. The basic requirements of marine plants are light, carbon dioxide and adequate mineral salts. Lighting should be of the maximum intensity and duration possible. Carbon dioxide is provided as a respiratory waste product by almost every living thing in the aquarium and the necessary mineral salts are best provided by a well-balanced algae fertilizer.

Halimeda tuna is a small green alga consisting of calcified green, fan-shaped blades joined together in chains. *Caulerpa verticillata* is a pretty, fern-like alga which sends its distinctive shoots off from a basal runner. *Codium* is a dark-green mass of branched tubular thalli and, in the author's experience, adapts to aquarium conditions better than any other large alga. Growth of all types can be aided by planting the holdfast (root) in coral sand or in gravel.

Yellow-striped Emerald Triggerfish *(Balistapus undulatus)*

An invertebrate-only aquarium. In the centre is a fully open Featherduster Worm (*Sabellastarte indica*) showing the feathery appendages used to trap the plankton on which the worm feeds. Above and to the left of this worm are smaller tube worms with similar parchment-like tubes protecting their bodies but with food-catching feathers arranged spirally. The tentacles are sensitive to water movement and are swiftly retracted at the approach of danger.

The small anemone at bottom centre is a grass-feeding coelenterate, unlike the filter-feeding polyps. It is usually enough to feed a 5–6 in diameter anemone once every other day with, for example, a half-inch piece of vitaminized prawn.

In the lower right-hand corner is a clam (*Tridacna* sp.) in an open, feeding position. The gelatinous tissue of the extended mantle contains embedded *Zooxanthellae* algae.

INDEX

ACKNOWLEDGEMENTS

Special acknowledgement is made to Jane Burton who undertook the commissioned photography for this book.

S. C. BISSEROT: 121B. RON BOARDMAN: 27T; 47; 50T; 50B; 58T. JANE BURTON: Front Jacket; 7; 15; 18; 20; 21; 22T; 22B; 23T; 23B; 26; 27B; 28; 29T; 30; 31; 32; 34B; 35; 36; 38T; 38B; 39; 40; 42; 43; 45; 46; 51; 52; 54; 55B; 57; 59; 60; 62; 63B; 64; 65T; 65B; 67; 68T; 68B; 70; 72T; 72BL; 72BR; 73TR; 73B; 75TL; 75R; 76; 86; 101T; 101B; 102TR; 105; 108T; 109; 111L; 111R; 113L; 114; 116B; 117B; 120T; 120B; 121T; 124B; 125; 128T; 129T; 129B; 130; 133B; 134T; 136–137; 138; 139T; 141. ALAN CUPIT: 44B; 58B; 63T; 79; 128B. A. VAN DEN NIEUWEN-HUIZEN: 29B; 49; 55T; 56; 73TL; 75CL. BARRY PENGILLEY: 14; 88; 95; 97; 102TL; 104T; 104B; 106; 107R; 108B; 110B; 112T; 113R; 116T; 118T; 118BL; 119; 123L; 124T; 127TR; 131B; 132T; 132B; 133T; 139B; 140. PICTUREPOINT: 10. GRAHAM PIZZEY: Back Jacket. ALLAN POWER: 102BR; 117T.

All the artwork (Hamlyn Group copyright) is by George Thompson.